RE

D1637108

MYSTERY

SCHOOL

KARYN K. MITCHELL, N.D., PH.D.

REIKI MYSTERY SCHOOL

Library of Congress Cataloging-in-Publication Data
Mitchell, Karyn
Reiki, Beyond the Usui System
ISBN 0-9640822-5-X
1. Healing 2. Alternative Medicine
94-075679

Mind Rivers Publishing
924 N. Daysville
Oregon, IL 61061
815-732-7150

Printed in the United States of America

2 3 4 5 6 7 8 9 10 11 12

Medical Disclaimer

The information in this book is for educational purposes only. It is not
intended to replace or contradict any advice given to you by your doctor
or healthcare specialist. The greatest powers that you have over dis-
ease are wisdom, Ki energy, and spiritual awareness. It is your Divine
right to manifest health, happiness, harmony, abundance, and peace in
your life. First, you must take responsibility for the wellness of your own
body, and empower yourself. Do not abdicate this power to anyone else!
In the end, only you can heal you on all levels: physical, mental, emotional, and spiritual. Reiki is not allopathic medicine, nor is it a religion.
It is a path of Love, the "road less traveled" that awakens the power and
purpose of the incarnate soul.

TABLE OF CONTENTS

With humble gratitude, I dedicate this book to the energy of Compassion, that all beings will be encouraged to embrace It and allow It to become their focus in greater understanding of Cosmic Awareness.

Karyn Mitchell

The past, present, and future are only illusions, however persistent. Albert Einstein

INTRODUCTION TO REIKI MYSTERY SCHOOL

A mystery school traditionally is a time or place where a student enters in to learn from a Master the ancient mystical secrets concerning life, death, immortality, healing, and mysteries withheld from the mainstream. These mystery teachings are passed down through the ages and shared only with those "who have ears that are ready to hear." In her book, The Secret Oral Teachings In Tibetan Buddhist Sects, Alexandra David-Neel reveals an interesting insight into the sharing and nature of these sacred teachings:

> "One may proclaim on the high road the Teachings considered secret, they will remain 'secret' for the individuals with dull minds who will hear what is said to them, and will grasp nothing of it but the sound.
> "It is not on the Master that the 'secret' depends but on the hearer. A Master can only be he (she) who opens the door: it is for the disciple to be capable of seeing what lies beyond. Teachers exist who are able to discern the degree of intellectual acuteness of those who desire their Teaching, and they reserve the detailed explanation of certain doctrines for those they judge able to understand them. It is thus that the deep Teachings, transmitted orally from Master to disciple for many generations, have been passed on and preserved from oblivion." (p. 3)

The Tibetans call these secret or sacred Teachings "Gsang wai Gdam Ngag." In this same book, Alexandra David-Neel tells an ancient story of Buddha:

> "Then the Buddha cast a supremely clairvoyant look over the world. He saw some beings whose spiritual eyes were hardly covered by thin dust. He saw some whose minds were keen and others whose minds were dull.
> "Just as in a pond, among lotus flowers born in the water, some do not emerge from the water and bloom in the depths, others grow to the surface of the water, and others emerge

from the water and the water does not wet their flowers, so the Buddha, casting His eyes on the world saw some beings whose minds were pure from the filth of the world, beings with keen minds and others with dull minds, beings of noble character, good listeners and bad. When He had seen these things he spoke to Brahma Sahampati, saying:

"Let the Gate of the Eternal be open to all! Let him who has ears to hear, hear!" (p. 6)

Who are we to judge who is open to the transmission of sacred Teachings? Buddha realized that these Teachings could only be understood by those who were truly ready for them. Like the beauty of the sacred Lotus blossoms, we are reminded that our roots are in the mud. It is our reaching upward lifetime after lifetime that brings us to the moment when we can not only seek and hear the Truth, but understand it. There are many places in time and space where we can seek the Truth, as nearly every culture throughout time has sought the Truth of our existence, or at least the secrets of life and death. Death becomes a transformational teacher for all of us.

In his poem, "On Death," Kahlil Gibran shares his perspective on the secret of life and death:

"You would know the secret of death. But how shall you find it unless you seek it in the heart of life?...
For life and death are one, even as the river and the sea are one.
In the depth of your hopes and desires lies your silent knowledge of the beyond ...
For what is it to die but to stand naked in the wind and to melt into the sun?
And what is to cease breathing, but to free the breath from its restless tides, that it may rise and expand and seek God unencumbered?
Only when we drink from the river of silence shall you indeed sing.
And when you have reached the mountain top, then you shall begin to climb.
And when the earth shall claim your limbs, then shall you truly dance."

It would require more than this one book and more than this one lifetime to share with you the esoteric teachings of even one ancient Mystery School. It is my hope only to bring to light energies from various Tibetan, Hindu, and other ancient traditions that I have discovered whose philosophies relate to some aspect of Reiki. These chapters also represent a lifelong journey that has personally led me into many fragrant fields of philosophy, religion, and esoteric studies. In this respect, it has always been my desire to first of all define and honor Traditional Reiki in its historical context, and secondly to provide a deeper understanding of its evolution or transformation as a viable healing model or alternative in the new millennium. Reiki must be as practical and applicable for us now as it was for Master Usui at the turn of the last century. I believe that there are many ways to ascend the spiritual mountain. Some are hazardously steep, and if you survive the journey, it can lead you to the summit more quickly, perhaps in just one lifetime, like that of the Tibetan's Vajrayana, or "Diamond Vehicle." There is also a path that is long and leisurely, and not particularly challenging in nature. It takes perhaps hundreds of lifetimes to ascend on this path. There is also a middle path, one that can challenge the soul but also allows the journeyer a respite from the arduous trek. This path may take fifty to one hundred lifetimes. A Journeyer generally chooses to vary the intensity of these experiences from one lifetime to the next. There are, in truth, as many paths and as much time as there are journeyers, but these three particular paths best demonstrate my point. From my studies, I have found that anyone who wishes to ascend their Sacred Mountain will do so, and the journey in and of itself may be all that matters. It is the journey that becomes the Master, the teacher, and the teachings.

Since I have received the gift of Reiki, I have found that there are many people ardently searching for their path. Some people are trapped, moving in the same circular pattern year after year, bored and uninspired to move beyond the circle.

They know the circle, and while it may be boring, it is comfortable for them. With humor, I say that there is generally a television at the center of this particular circle rather than a sacred mountain. Some tread the same circular path until a type of death occurs, either physical or spiritual, for they have dug such a deep trench from their footsteps that they can no longer see the blue of the sky or the illumination from the sun's rays. What lies beyond the rut of this circle is the unknown, and this unrealized potential or perhaps self love poses a threat to their reality.

We have before us at the unfolding of the new millennium, the challenge to advance spiritually and heal, not just as an individual, but as a world society. The Tibetans call this harsh time the "Kaliyuga." What one country does affects the global community, affects us all. It is imperative that we recognize that our elected alienation from Mother Earth Herself alienates us from ourselves and our own healing. In Tibetan medicine, the tantras reveal the embodiment of one known as the Medicine Buddha, "Bhaishajaguru." This Medicine Buddha is surrounded by aspects of Nature: trees, herbs, and medicinal plants, including teas, cordyceps, musk, angelica, licorice, ginseng, mugwort, cardamom, camphor, and cinnamon, healing stones and jewels including gold, silver, ruby, turquoise and coral. These stones are ground into what is called precious pills or "rinchen rilbus." The Medicine Buddha is heralded as the Blue or Aquamarine-Light Healing Buddha, as he emanates a radiating blue light from his aura that releases the dark energies of negative emotions and physical disharmony. Tibetan physicians begin each day by seeing themselves as the image of the Medicine Buddha. They invoke his presence in the following manner:

"As all sentient beings, infinite as space are encompassed by the compassion of the Master of Remedies, may I too become their guide...may I quickly attain the powers of the Medicine Buddha, Bhaishajyaguru, and lead all beings into his enlightened realm." [1]

1.The Tibetan Art of Healing, Ian Baker, Chronicle Books, San Francisco, p.33

From this perspective, then, it remains the task of the healer to assume the energy to "liberate all beings from the miseries of ignorance and disease."[2] In Tibetan medicine, disease is "attributed to a basic ignorance of the interdependent origin of all phenomenon and the true nature of the self."[3] We must also assume, as healers, two things if we accept this Tibetan healing model: 1.) We are capable of understanding our own "true nature" as a part of the Greater Cosmic Whole, and 2.) We are capable of educating and leading others out of ignorance and into this same understanding.

It is as Dickens would say, "The best of times and the worst of times..." As we approach the new millennium, the least we could do is take a look ahead, or at least take a look up. That Sacred Mountaintop is always closer than we can imagine. The Ancient Ones who have gone before us teach us that there is a way to healing and Enlightenment, and that each of us can find it if we make it a focus of our attention and life. It does not have to be difficult unless that is what we need for us to sufficiently appreciate it.

I hope that this book brings some insight or illumination to your own path and into understanding yourself as a part of the Greater Cosmic Whole. While this information represents the accumulation of my years of sifting through various sacred traditions, please remember that I do not represent your Truth. Blessings to you and all you touch with your compassionate heart as you journey on your own path toward Truth.

---

2. <u>The Tibetan Art of Healing</u>, Ian Baker, Chronicle Books, San Francisco, p.35
3. Ibid p. 58

THE BRAIN AND ITS HEALING POTENTIAL

"Though the mind cannot directly produce physical form, negative feelings such as envy, hatred, and fear, when they become habitual, are capable of starting organic changes within our bodies."
Dr. Lobsang Rapgay, from The Tibetan Art of Healing

Where is pain first born? Is it born first in the Physical Body, the Mental Body, the Emotional Body, or the Spiritual Body? Perhaps a look at brain wave frequencies can assist us in understanding the function of the brain as it relates to states of consciousness. Brain wave frequencies, called Hertz, are a unit of frequency equal to one cycle per second.

"It has been discovered that different states of consciousness produce different brain frequencies. During waking consciousness, the frequencies of the brain waves emitted start from 14 Hertz. This area of frequency is called beta rhythm. In a state of relaxation or light sleep, the brain wave frequency slows down to 7-14 Hertz. This frequency range, called alpha rhythm, is induced by relaxation through self hypnosis and other suggestive methods. In waking consciousness, the theta rhythm, which has a frequency of 4-7 hertz, is only reached in certain situations, such as deep, healing meditation. The frequencies between 1-4 hertz, the delta rhythm, is reached only in deep sleep. In that state, the waking consciousness is completely switched off."

"With reference to the principle, 'As within, so without', it is possible to offer the brain certain frequencies it knows so that it shifts according to the principle of resonance into the desired vibrational state. Therefore, the vibrational changes induced from the outside will have an effect on the inside, namely, a change of consciousness." [4]

---

4. Esogentics, Peter Mandel, Energetic-Verlag CmbH-Sulzbach/Tanus, Germany, 1993, p. 88

BRAIN WAVE FREQUENCY		
BETA	14 + HERTZ	WAKING CONSCIOUSNESS
ALPHA	7-14 HERTZ	RELAXATION OR LIGHT SLEEP
THETA	4- 7 HERTZ	DEEP HEALING MEDITATION
DELTA	1- 4 HERTZ	DEEP SLEEP

If a person desires to heal, then, it is evident that healing occurs at the change of consciousness level. That is the Deep Healing Meditation Level of Theta, or 4-7 Hertz. I feel that our bodies are so bombarded by outside frequencies such as radio or EMF frequencies, that our incarnate bodies in our present technological age find it difficult to achieve this vibrational level of 4-7 Hertz naturally as they once did. An energy field must then be created, one which I choose to call the "UNISONIUM," or becoming one in harmony. This field may be created by the individual through various methods, or may be created in conjunction with another as in the healer-healee model, or the director-healee model. Active participation on some level by the individual is a great force desired in the healing process. It activates a greater flow of Ki through the chakras, and removes negative energy or thought forms blocking the chakras. Throughout recorded history, these three methodologies of creating the vibrational field shift have been alluded to or practiced in some way, either through the auspices of religion through prayer, shamanic tradition and the attainment of ecstasy, through the ancient vehicle in many cultures of chanting, drumming, or whirling into the altered state of transcendent reality, or the transfer of energy directly or indirectly through therapeutic applications of magnetic or spiritual healing.

Possible samples of the three models might be viewed as follows:

MODEL	VEHICLE
SELF INDUCED:	Reiki Self-treatment, Prayer, Visualization, Ecstasy*
HEALER-HEALEE:	Hands-on Reiki, Therapeutic Touch, Pranic Healing
HEALEE-DIRECTOR:	Absentia Reiki Healing, Magnetic Healing, Hypnotherapy

*Note: The word, ecstasy derives from the Greek word, "ekstasis", which means "to displace or drive out of one's senses". It also means, "the trance, frenzy, or rapture associated with mystic or prophetic exaltation." (The American Heritage Dictionary of the English Language)

In Reiki, we recognize two Precepts. Precept implicates the notion of "practice" or "intention" rather than moral law. The first Precept is: "For healing to occur, there must be a change in consciousness." Perhaps the reflection upon frequency and vibrational shift leads us to a new understanding, if not a different paradigm concerning the healing model. Perhaps the change in consciousness involves the raising of the vibrational frequency that shifts old habits. The second Precept is, "There must be an exchange of energy for healing to occur." Considering Transformational Reiki™, or Trans-Reiki™, which means, "beyond the form" or beyond the physical body, then, the two Reiki Precepts may assume a new perspective or expanded intention:

TRANSFORMATIONAL REIKI PRECEPTS:
THERE MUST BE A FREQUENCY CHANGE FOR HEALING TO OCCUR.
THERE MUST BE A FIELD EXCHANGE OF ENERGY CREATED BETWEEN HEALEE-HEALER FOR HEALING TO OCCUR.

In other words, both the change of consciousness and the energy exchange become the responsibility not so much of the Reiki Practitioner, but rather that of the client or healee. The Reiki Practitioner is merely the Way, the conduit, the channel to this new level of energy attainment. If there is not a change of consciousness, I have found, time and time again, that the same or similar dis-ease will return. Old patterns of thought and habit must be somehow released from the mental body grid within each sentient cell. We must heal the mind and the cellular consciousness that contains the mental body grid to liberate the energies essential for healing the other bodies: the Spiritual, the Emotional, and the Physical. This holds the key for the Way (or the Tao) of Transformational Healing: We can access the mind through the spirit via the Interdimensional Body. The Unisonium is the map. The map is represented later in the text of this book. We begin our journey into Transformational Reiki by studying first the Subtle Body Chakras, and then affirming the Transformational Chakras.

SUBTLE BODY CHAKRAS AND PATTERNS FOR HEALING

Patterns are created in the vortex of each chakra as they experience life in the physical world. All 88,000 chakras of the physical system imprint patterns of health and dis-ease in this process. If the pattern affirms positive life processes and soul growth, then each chakra spins in harmony with itself and all others. If negative energy collects around particular life issues related to the associate chakra, then what has been called by most, "blocks," occur. I choose to call these obstacles healing opportunities, as the clearing of them always lead to deepening knowledge and awareness. Some esoteric teachings consider these to be lessons about life that we must experience. In Pranic Healing they consider such impacting of the chakra to be the creation of "Webs." As the webs or blocks are cleared, then harmony is restored.

THE SUBTLE BODY CHAKRAS

SAHASRARA   1,000 PETAL LOTUS   CROWN CENTER
ENERGY OF ACTION

AJNA   2 PETALS   THIRD EYE
ENERGY OF KNOWLEDGE

VISUDDHA   16 PETALS   THROAT CENTER
ENERGY OF KNOWLEDGE

ANAHATA   12 PETALS   HEART CENTER
ENERGY OF COMPASSION

MANIPURA   10 PETALS   SOLAR PLEXUS
ENERGY OF WILL

SVADHISHTHANA 6 PETALS   SACRAL (BELOW NAVEL)
ENERGY OF WILL

MULADHARA   4 PETALS   ROOT (BASE OF SPINE)
ENERGY OF WILL

Master Hawayo Takata worked primarily with the glands of the Endocrine system, as she so learned from Master Hayashi in her healing treatments. Traditionally, it is said, she did not treat the limbs of the body, as they were void of gland sites. The treatment of the chakras of the subtle body correspond approximately to the following glands of the endocrine system.

GLANDS OF THE ENDOCRINE SYSTEM

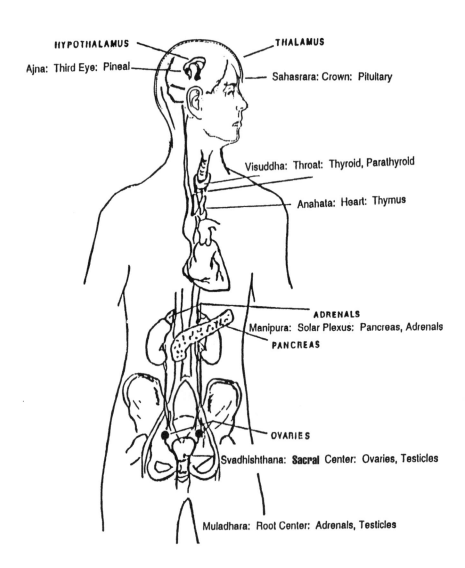

HYPOTHALAMUS

Ajna: Third Eye: Pineal

THALAMUS

Sahasrara: Crown: Pituitary

Visuddha: Throat: Thyroid, Parathyroid

Anahata: Heart: Thymus

ADRENALS

Manipura: Solar Plexus: Pancreas, Adrenals

PANCREAS

OVARIES

Svadhishthana: Sacral Center: Ovaries, Testicles

Muladhara: Root Center: Adrenals, Testicles

SELF-HEALING AFFIRMATIONS
©1995 Karyn Mitchell

You may use these affirmations, or your own, for twenty one days or more to release past-life karma that may be stored in the Physical, Mental, Emotional, and Spiritual Bodies. **Self-Healing is essential to spiritual growth as well as physical healing.**

Affirm: "I have chosen this physical body for a reason. I acknowledge that I exist beyond the limitations of my physical body. If there is any karma or karmic patterns stored in my body or in any part of me, I now request guidance in releasing these patterns and for any change of consciousness that is required for healing and manifesting my life to complete my soul's purpose in this lifetime. So be it!"

CROWN CHAKRA: The color is violet. Visualize violet energy flowing through you as you place your hands upon the Crown Center. This is the Center where we manifest our spiritual destiny. **Affirm:** "I am a Spiritual Being living a physical life. I am fulfilling my spiritual destiny."

AJNA (THIRD EYE) Center: Visualize the color indigo. This is the Center where we learn to trust the Universe. **Affirm:** "I trust my intuition and psychic awareness flows to me effortlessly."

THROAT CENTER: Visualize the color blue. This is the Center of self expression, where you speak your Truth free of fear. Perhaps you have been afraid of how others would judge you. You must love yourself enough to express who you really are. **Affirm:** "I speak my Truth free of fear."

HIGH HEART CENTER: Visualize turquoise that contains the color gold. This is the center of self-love. It is easier to love others. Open your heart to yourself and to any aspect of yourself that you may have been rejecting such as your Inner Child or your Critical Parent. Dissolve them into the Light of your High Heart. **Affirm:** "I unconditionally love and accept myself and all that I am."

HEART CENTER: Visualize emerald green. This is the Center for unconditional love for others. Forgiveness is an important energy for healing the Heart Center. **Affirm:** "I love, forgive, and accept others." (You may list specific names as needed for healing forgiveness.)

SOLAR PLEXUS: Visualize clear yellow. This is your power center. It is associated with the Throat Center, and is greatly affected by your past. If you have been abused or manipulated by others, you may consider treating the Throat and Solar Plexus together. This **affirmation** is: "I now reclaim any power lost, stolen, or given away to others throughout my history." The Solar Plexus **affirmation** alone is: "I am a powerful loving soul incarnate. I channel the flame of power through my Heart Center."

SACRAL CENTER: Visualize clear orange. This is the center of your identity. You have chosen the features of your body, including male or female for a reason. **Affirm:** "I honor who I am, and I affirm my identity as female (or male)."

ROOT CENTER: Visualize clear red. This is the center of survival. More importantly, the root center allows us to actualize our soul's purpose in physical form. It grounds us to the Earth Plane. **Affirm:** "I live my soul's purpose and am grounded to the healing energies of the Earth."

KNEES: Visualize a clear or colored cylinder of Light. The knees are said to store our fear of death and the ego. **Affirm:** "Death is only a door. I channel my ego through my heart."

ANKLES: Visualize a clear or colored cylinder of Light. The ankles allow us to move forward in life and assist us in affirming change. **Affirm:** "I move forward in life. I embrace change."

TRANSFORMATIONAL CHAKRA AFFIRMATIONS

Assist in the release of Negative Patterns that may be impacting your own chakras as you administer Self Treatment. These could also translate into the Quick Treatment, Reiki Boost, or table treatment modalities for others whom you bless with Reiki.

ROOT CENTER: RED: I move beyond survival and into living my Soul's Purpose.

SACRAL CENTER: ORANGE: I have selected my gender to actualize my potential in this lifetime.

SOLAR PLEXUS: YELLOW: I channel all power through my Heart Center. I now release all inappropriate ties and cords from any who would manipulate me past, present, and future.

LEYDES CENTER: SAFFRON: I reset my biological time clock. I choose to live at the age of____and I now ordain my body to demonstrate this.

HEART CENTER: EMERALD GREEN: I love and accept others unconditionally.

HIGH HEART CENTER: TURQUOISE: I love and accept myself unconditionally.

THROAT: BLUE: I live my truth free of fear.

AJNA (THIRD EYE): INDIGO: I trust my truth and my intuition.

CROWN: VIOLET: I am a spiritual being manifesting a divine physical life.

SOUL STAR: SILVER: I transcend my lower ego.

TAO CENTER: GOLD: I am one with all of life.

INTERDIMENSIONAL CENTER: PEARL WHITE: I exist in all planes and in all dimensions, in all time and space simultaneously. I am limitless reality.

SEVEN SACRED BODIES:
TRANSFORMATIONAL AFFIRMATIONS

PHYSICAL: I honor my physical body and am sensitive to its needs.

MENTAL: Divine, positive consciousness dwells within each cell of my body.

EMOTIONAL: I allow myself to feel the reality of my existence.

SPIRITUAL: I release all concepts and patterns that are not serving my Highest Good.

COSMIC: I transcend desire and communicate through my Higher Self energy.

LIGHT: My Ki is united with all that is.

INTERDIMENSIONAL: My Ki is unlimited.

THE AFFIRMATION APPLICATIONS

In Reiki Level One class, I always relate what I call my "Spock Theory." That is, we are born with all bodies integrated, like the four primary fingers held together tightly on the hand. The index finger symbolically represents the Spiritual Body. ("Pointing directly at your own heart, there you find Buddha.") The second finger represents the Emotional Body. The ring finger represents the Physical Body, and the little finger the Mental Body. These fingers (representing the four bodies) begin to separate through time and the fire of life. We separate from our other bodies to cope with our environment and society.

We learn that it is not socially acceptable to laugh in a boisterous manner, or cry in public, so we learn to disassociate from our feelings. We learn that it is not culturally appropriate to share our spirituality, so we separate from our spiritual nature. It seems that what is most honored is the Mental Body in our Western culture, and the Physical Body only if it looks good and doesn't cause us any trouble. It is, after all, impolite to have a cold in public. So there develops a great split after awhile. The "live long and prosper" pose...where the two fingers split from the others in the middle of the hand, is indicative of the Western Culture Split. The Mental and Physical Bodies split from the Emotional and Spiritual Bodies. Eventually the Emotional and Spiritual Bodies may atrophy from disuse. This doesn't mean your fingers fall off, however. What it does indicate is that most people in our culture attempt to live their lives with half of their Third Dimensional bodies. They lead a Bi-Body existence. It is not healthy. It creates the space for disease. Life becomes survival, and the soul's purpose is focused on the negative aspects of attaining material wealth and property. These activities function as a secure anchor for the Bi-Body, creating the negative side effect energies of worry, debt, fear, and jealousy. But true life is much more. Integration with all four of our 3-D Bodies is essential to a happy, healthy life in this Earth Plane. Thus the affirmations of the four Third Dimensional Bodies is important. "Physical: I honor my physical body and am sensitive to its needs." This affirmation also implies that excess acquisition does not add to security. The body does not need excess material property. Too many extra "things" in the life creates a heavy weight that impairs access to the Spiritual Body. Consider "clearing" extra baggage from your life. George Carlin, the comedian, created an entire routine about "stuff." I know people who are fearful to leave home because of their "stuff" or without their "stuff." We are not our "stuff", although American advertisers would have us believe otherwise. At the Mental Body Level, we affirm, "Divine, positive consciousness dwells within each cell of my body." Our Mental Body is not just our brain, and our thoughts and personality are not separate from the whole of us. Acceptance of and integration with all energies of the Self is essential for balance. Our Mental Body defines us chronologically through the vehicle of our thoughts programming each cell. We are who and what we think we are. It is essential that we feed our Self only positive, youthful thoughts to nurture our soul.

Those who cultivate integration with the Emotional and Spiritual Bodies learn that there is much more to them. The Emotional Body Affirmation is: "I allow myself to feel the reality of my existence." There is no need to disassociate from what you feel. It is a major part of your Truth. It is the emotions that allow us to store memory. That is why people experience repressed memories, as they have been labeled. The Mental Body disassociated from the Emotional Body because of trauma or betrayal, and the memory is displaced. These are not always completely lost, just sometimes temporarily misfiled. When it is the appropriate time for healing concerning the violation, then the missing chip falls into place. The repressed memory surfaces. The Emotional Body downloads its information to the Mental Body. Thus, the affirmation becomes a combination of the two: "I allow myself to feel the reality of my existence through the Divine Consciousness that dwells within each cell of my body." The integration of the first three bodies then leads to the Spiritual Body affirmation: "I release all concepts and patterns that are not serving my highest good." True healing takes place. The individual learns that they are indeed Spiritual Bodies choosing to lead a physical life. What happened in the past no longer creates havoc in the Divine moment of the present. They are ready to integrate with their other Bodies as well, to develop a new level of awareness and existence beyond the past and all material reality. This is the Cosmic Body awakening, where there is recognition of the Soul Star Connection. You are a part of all that exists, there is no separation. It is the awakening of this Center that may prove to be painful for many. As your consciousness raises, it is difficult to live with feet in both worlds, so to speak. Compassion becomes your focus. In other words, you may adopt a vegetarian lifestyle in order not to inflict pain, suffering, or death upon other sentient creatures of which you are a part. It becomes painful to witness trees being cut down or uprooted for new housing developments or shopping malls. It is even difficult to watch violent programs or listen to harsh language. In other words, it is a challenge to live a sensitive life in a world where many choose to ignore the Spiritual-Emotional Bodies. This is the difficulty that many artists have had throughout history. It also leads to addictive behaviors as such deep sensitivity cannot easily cope. You feel like you are out of sync with the rest of the human race. But would you go back to the Bi-Body existence? I have asked many this question, in somewhat different terms, and the answer is always no. Higher consciousness may hurt at times, but transcending the lower ego leads to an incredible power and wisdom. It is "living within the jaws of the serpent" as Buddha was once portrayed. You choose to live your spiritual life in the midst of a non-spiritual reality, surrounded by drama and chaos, your Spiritual Self flourishes inspite of it all. The Cosmic Body Affirmation is: "I transcend desire and communicate through my Higher Self Energy." Such honest communication truly scares those who choose to live in mass-consciousness reality. They cannot relate to your Higher Self. You are not the same old you. You realize that it becomes increasingly difficult to be around individuals who are negative, so you begin to develop new friends, a lifestyle free of negativity. You meditate and tune in to the Cosmic Music of your own soul. Your Cosmic Body has integrated with the other four bodies.

As your frequency raises, your High Heart Center opens and triangulates with two other major heart centers. The vibrational colors reflected in these three major core centers are: Emerald Green, Light Pink, and Turquoise...much like the radiant blending of the stone Tourmaline. These connect with the now open and illumined Soul Star Center to create a great pyramid of energy that leads to the awareness of the Tao Center. As this center opens, it reveals to us our pre-birth into the physical realm of existence. The Light Body Awareness emerges, and the affirmation is, "My Ki is united with All That Is." We were and are a part of the Golden Ray, the Creator and the Creation. We co-create, we manifest, our existence, our reality. We live our Soul's Purpose in complete harmony with all life around us. We transcend judgment of others and self-judgment, for to judge is to create separation. There is no me-you. It is the Divine incarnation of "We." And "We" are an unlimited force in the Omniverse. At this Level, we are ready for the next step, integration with the Interdimensional Body. I feel that at this time, we become aware of the potential of the Bodhisattva. Life is not survival of the fittest. Truth transcends survival. The Earth is no longer viewed as a predatory planet. "Ki is unlimited," is the affirmation of the Interdimensional Body. The Buddha is in you, the Buddha is you. "Budh" is the Sanskrit root which means "to wake up, be awake." In the ancient literature of the Vedas, around the second millennium B.C.E., this term also implied the "recovery of consciousness." The Interdimensional Body has always been there, we have just not been aware of it. As the saying goes, "When the student is ready, the Teacher comes." We are the teacher. Buddha transcended his teachers. In fact, legend holds that his two teachers, Udraka and Arada Kalama made their transition just days following the enlightenment of Buddha. We must all gain enlightenment on our own. It is much like transition or death, a journey to be taken singularly. It is as Kahlil Gibran stated, "If he, the teacher, is indeed wise, he does not bid you enter the house of his wisdom, but rather leads you to the threshold of your own."

Buddha (Siddhartha Gautama) was born 567 B.C.E. at the foothills of the Himalayas, and died at the age of 80 in the town of Kushinagara. It is believed that he was poisoned. Like Christ, nothing was written of his discourses until after his death. What was later written by his "Bhikkhus" or followers, created the three baskets of the Buddhist canon. These were: the "Sutras" (discourses or sacred words), the "Vinaya" or 250 monastic rules, and the "Abhidharma," or sacred psychology. Contained in these were the concepts of the "Four Noble Truths." I will attempt to paraphrase them.

THE FOUR NOBLE TRUTHS

I.) Life is "Dukkha." Painful by nature, unsatisfying, impermanent so unreliable.

2.) This Truth differentiates between the inevitable pains of life and the extra pain created by the mind as it struggles rather than accommodates.

3.) This Truth holds the promise that peace of mind and a contented heart are not dependent upon external circumstances.

4.) The Eightfold Path of Practice. A commitment to transformation. This includes:

> **RIGHT MINDFULNESS**
> **RIGHT UNDERSTANDING**
> **RIGHT CONCENTRATION**
> **RIGHT ASPIRATION**
> **RIGHT LIVELIHOOD**
> **RIGHT SPEECH**
> **RIGHT EFFORT**
> **RIGHT ACTION**

The EIGHTFOLD PATH OF PRACTICE shares much of the same intention and energy as the REIKI PRINCIPLES. "Just for Today" of the Reiki Principles reflects "Right Mindfulness" and "Right Concentration" of the Eightfold Path. "Do not anger" encompasses "Right Speech," but holds elements of all of the commitments. "Do not worry" reflects "Right Aspiration," but elements of all of the others also. "Earn your living honestly" reflects "Right Livelihood" and "Right Effort." "Honor your parents, teachers, and elders" reflects "Right Understanding," and "Show gratitude to every living thing" is definitely "Right

Action." The word "Right" implies personal resposibility to Karmic-free behavior. No word for guilt exists in Sanskrit. The Eightfold Path of Practice is written with an implied subject, just as the Reiki Principles. The implied subject is the You of your highest actualized self:

REIKI PRINCIPLES
Just for today (You) do not anger.
Just for today (You) do not worry.
(You) Honor your parents, teachers, and elders.
(You) Earn your living honestly.
(You) Show gratitude to every living thing.

The Reiki Principles, like the Eightfold Path of Practice are agents of focus and change. They are transformational in nature and by design, as they were presented to humanity by Enlightened Beings. I suggest that you utilize the Principles as a mantra of sorts. "Mantra" in Sanskrit means thought form, or mind and body united. Recite it several times a day to yourself until it acts like a catalyst for positive change in your daily life. The sounds, repeated constantly through time create a powerful vibrational energy. When we live right, we raise our vibration to a place of harmony with the Universe. I know a man, a college professor, who was plagued by anger. Other people made him so angry that he could barely tolerate being around them. One day at the gym, he affirmed the Reiki Principles to himself as he performed his routine exercises. It became a habit. The words fell into the movements. Soon, his life began to change dramatically. His negative attitudes evolved into more positive thoughts and actions. He began to make new friends with old acquaintances and colleagues. He told me that he had discovered that his anger was not so much with others as with himself. The Reiki Principles changed his vibration through his Mental-Physical Bodies first, and eventually his Emotional-Spiritual Bodies as well. They are a dynamic catalyst for change, but we must make them a focus, a commitment. For twenty one consecutive days, give yourself the gift of Mantra Meditation with the Traditional Reiki Principles or as they are listed below. Recite them just three times a day, or more if you choose to. Make them a song with any tune that you prefer to sing. If you are so inspired, keep a journal of the change that they create in you, or how your days are different. Perhaps those changes will be subtle at first, but if you truly embrace the Principles in your daily life, you will begin to transcend negativity. Your vibration raises. The "do nots" become past tense for you. Living in the only reality, the moment, you find that you are free to say:

THE TRANSFORMATIONAL REIKI PRINCIPLES

Now I am free of anger. (*I accept Joy in my life.)

Now I am free of worry. (*My life is fulfilling.)

I honor the wisdom in myself and all others. (Honor Higher Consciousness.)

I earn my living honestly. (*I enjoy my chosen dharma.)

I am grateful for and honor all life. (*And All That Is.)

The asterisk is my own personal addition to my Mantra. If you are attempting to program through the mind for change, it is important not to utilize negative concepts such as "do not." That is why I have substituted for this mantra purpose the words "free of" for "do not." I hope that Master Usui finds this substitution acceptable. If you prefer, utilize the traditional Reiki Principles. Whatever works spiritually for you is best. Use your discernment. Be prepared to cultivate joy in your life, for it is a positive side effect.

Thich Nhat Hanh has developed his version of "The Five Wonderful Precepts," a translation of the precepts presented by Buddha over two thousand five hundred years ago. He states:

"These precepts can perform miracles. The moment we decide to receive them, a transformation already occurs in us that touches everything. The foundation of all precepts is mindfulness. We begin each precept with the awareness of a particular problem, saying, 'Aware of...'Then instead of saying, 'Don't do this' or 'don't do that,' we say, 'I am determined to do this, I am determined to do that.'" [5]

"THE FIVE WONDERFUL PRECEPTS"

I. "Aware of the suffering caused by the destruction of life, I vow to cultivate compassion and learn ways to protect the lives of people, animals, and plants. I am determined not to kill, not to let others kill, and not to condone any act of killing in the world, in my thinking and in my way of life.

2. Aware of the suffering caused by exploitation, social injustice, stealing, and oppression, I vow to cultivate loving kindness and learn ways to work for the well-being of people, animals, and plants. I vow to practice generosity by sharing my time, energy, and material resources with those who are in real need. I am determined not to steal and not to possess anything that should belong to others. I will respect the property of others, but will prevent others from profiting from human suffering or the suffering of other species on Earth.

3. Aware of the suffering caused by sexual misconduct, I vow to cultivate responsibility and learn ways to protect the safety and integrity of individuals, couples, families, and society. I am determined not to engage in sexual relations without love and a long-term commitment. To preserve the happiness of myself and others, I will do everything in my power to protect children from sexual abuse and to prevent couples and families from being broken by sexual misconduct.

4. Aware of the suffering caused by unmindful speech and the inability to listen to others, I vow to cultivate loving speech and deep listening in order to bring joy and happiness to others and relieve others of their suffering. Knowing that words can create happiness or suffering, I vow to learn to speak truthfully, with words that inspire self-confidence, joy, and hope. I

---

5. "Mindfulness Bell", Issue 6, Spring 1992, Berkeley, CA., p.1

am determined not to spread news that I do not know to be certain and not to criticize or condemn things of which I am not sure. I will refrain from uttering words that can cause division or discord, or that can cause the family or community to break. I will make all efforts to reconcile and resolve all conflicts, however small.

5. Aware of the suffering caused by unmindful consumption, I vow to cultivate good health, both physical and mental, for myself, my family, and my society by practicing mindful eating, drinking, and consuming. I vow to ingest only items that preserve peace, well-being, and joy in my body, in my consciousness, and in the collective consciousness of my family and society. I am determined not to use alcohol or any other intoxicant or to ingest foods or other items that contain toxins, such as certain TV programs, magazines, books, films, and conversations. I am aware that to damage my body or my consciousness with these poisons is to betray my ancestors, my parents, my society, and future generations. I will work to transform violence, fear, anger, and confusion in myself and in society by practicing a diet for myself and for society. I understand that a proper diet is crucial for self-transformation and for the transformation of society."[6]

Practices or "Limbs" are also presented in the Hindu considerations of Yoga:

The Eight Limbs of Classical Yoga
1.) Yama: The ethics. Nonviolence.
2.) Niyama. Discipline
3.) Asana. Postures that link to higher truths.
4.) Pranayama. Breath of Heaven and Breath of Earth forms life.
5.) Pratahara. Freedom of distraction of the senses.
6.) Dharana. Centering the mind.
7.) Dhyana. Meditation.
8.) Samadhi. Transcending time and space.

6."The Mindfulness Bell", Issue 5, Autumn 1991, Berkeley, CA., p. 6

DHARMA: THE WAY

"I believe a work of grass is no less than the journey-work of stars." Walt Whitman

Zen Master Thich Nhat Hanh explains his awareness of the principle of mindfulness: "The Chinese character for mindfulness has two components: heart, or mind, and present moment. To be mindful means to be fully present in the moment--not one part of you washing the dishes while another part is wondering when the work will be finished."[7]

Those who love cats will agree with me that they are teachers of The Way. Zen is their very essence. Just observe as they set about the awesome task of cleaning their fur. Perhaps it would be more appropriate to call such an undertaking a nurturing of the soul. It is like the Seventh Precept of fourteen offered to the Tiep Hien or the Order of Inner Being by Thich Nhat Hanh:

"Do not lose yourself in dispersion and in your surroundings. Practice mindful breathing to come back to what is happening in the present moment. Be in touch with what is wondrous, refreshing, and healing both inside and around you. Plant seeds of joy, peace, and understanding in yourself in order to facilitate the work of transformation in the depths of your consciousness."[8]

A cat is so absorbed in the cleaning ritual that they become one with the event. As they begin to close their eyes, you sense that they are dissolving deeper and deeper into their own experience. Oftentimes purring accompanies this ritual. This is their mantra--the song sung by the soul as it expresses its harmony with life. Do you sing when you work? Does your work make you sing? Poet-philosopher Kahlil Gibran wrote: "Work is love made visible. And if you cannot work with love but only with distaste, it is better that you should leave your work and sit at the gate of the temple and take alms of those

---

7. "The Mindfulness Bell", Issue 5, Autumn 1991, Berkeley, CA., p. 6
8. Interbeing, Fourteen Guidelines for Engaged Buddhism, Thich Nhat Hanh, Parallax Press, Berkeley, CA., 1987, p. 18

who work with joy." Meditate with your cat the next time they partake of their ritual of cleaning; feel as your own aura is affected by the soothing vibrations that a cat shares with all whom it trusts to hold audience. Translate the cat's teachings into your own life. A cat does not worry about material objects or their life in the future. Tomorrow simply does not exist. Focus mindful attention on all that you do:

"The practice of mindfulness is not reserved for the meditation cushion. It should be brought to bear on what is happening at any and every moment. Needless to say, our usual condition is a kind of waking dream. We are almost totally distracted, lost in trains of unreflective thought and fantasy, which are interwoven with beguiling emotional sub-themes. These move reactively through life according to conditioned habit-patterns. We may be habitual grumblers, for instance, who at every pretext launch into embittered diatribes with all the predictability of Pavlov's dogs.

If we are able to wake up, if only occasionally and for a few moments at first, stand back from the ongoing drama of our lives and take an objective look at the habit patterns in which we are caught, then their compulsive hold over us begins to loosen. We dis-identify from them; that is, we begin to see that those thoughts and feelings are not us. They come along accidentally. They are neither an organic part of us nor are we obliged to follow them."[9]

It is much like the Buddhist saying, "Before enlightenment, chop wood, carry water. After enlightenment, chop wood, carry water." But we do so with a higher vibration!

"The Buddha once said that the problem of life and death is itself the problem of mindfulness. Whether or not one is alive depends on whether one is mindful." (Thich Nhat Hanh, The Miracle of Mindfulness, p. 62,) Mindfulness is also a great gift to others. The Tao Te Ching states:

"In dwelling, live close to the ground.
In thinking, keep to the simple.
In conflict, be fair and generous.
In governing, don't try to control.
In work, do what you enjoy.
In family life, be completely present."

9. John Snelling, The Buddist Handbook, (Rochester, VT, Inner Traditions, 1991) p. 55

If you are truly present with your friends, your Reiki clients, or your family, you are more than just a body in the chair. You are there for them and with them physically, mentally, emotionally, and spiritually as well. You are mindful of all of these aspects of them as well. You trust and acknowledge their Highest Good and are free of fear for their future, for you know that it is ordained by them. Rather than give negative energy to the fearful parting words, "drive carefully," or "be careful," release those that you love with the blessing to "be mindful." This implies that you wish them to enjoy and be present with each and every moment of their lives. Mindfulness contains, by its very nature, the element of caring and compassion. "Look at other beings with the eyes of compassion," is from the Lotus Sutra. It is also a core teaching in other religious contexts, most notably Judaism and Christianity. Jesus embodied Compassion just as surely as the Avalokitesvara (Kuan Yin, the Goddess of Compassion) of Buddha did. This is the I-Thou relationship of Buber; the unity in Christ of Merton:

"Love, of course, means something much more than mere sentiment, much more than token favours and perfunctory almsdeeds. Love means an interior and spiritual identification with one's brother, so that he is not regarded as an 'object' to 'which' one 'does good.' The fact is that good done to another as to an object is of little or no spiritual value. Love takes one's neighbour as one's other self, and loves him with all the immense humility and discretion and reserve and reverence without which no one can presume to enter into the sanctuary of another's subjectivity. From such love all authoritarian brutality, all exploitation, domineering and condescension must necessarily be absent." [10]

There is an ancient story that I learned in Shiatsu Class. I will share it with you as best I remember it. It seems that in China, there was a woman, recently married, who found her mother-in-law to be intolerable. As the days, months, and years transpired, the situation seemed to deteriorate. Finally, the young woman sought assistance from the local sage. She truly wished her Mother-in-law dead, and so desired advice in

---

10. Lawrence Cunningham, Thomas Merton, Spiritual Master, (Mahwah, NJ, 1992), p. 275

hastening the process. The wise sage, after pondering for a moment replied, "Allow me to teach you how to perform Shiatsu. In time, that should do the trick. But you must perform this ritual every day for 180 days with your mother-in-law. That is the only way that it will work." The young woman returned home that very day and commenced the Shiatsu treatments, believing that it would eventually kill her mother-in-law. After five months, the sorrowful young woman returned to the wise sage. "Wise One," she said, "You must teach me how to reverse this process. I have grown quite fond of my mother-in-law, and she of me. I cannot bear to think of being without her." The young woman broke into tears. The wise sage smiled. "Then this is what you must do. You must offer her Shiatsu for the rest of her life." And the young woman did.

I believe that this story could translate into a compassionate act in any language. The sage in this story knew the ultimate truth in compassion, and shared its lesson in a most illuminating way. The young woman had a change in consciousness, as we say in Reiki. The wise sage, a healer, allowed her this opportunity, assisting her to find her own way to the truth. Yasutani Roshi once said, "The fundamental delusion of humanity is to suppose that I am here and you are out there." Compassion teaches us that we are all one and the same energy. It is one of the most difficult realities for us to contend with in our Western Culture. We are so focused on do-ing that we forget about be-ing. So it follows form that we forget that others are be-ings as well, rather than do-ings. We must learn to treat all in our path with compassion. I am teaching myself to silently say, "I love you as I love me," as I meet others in the world. It presupposes that I am capable of unconditional self-love and acceptance, and then translating that process into oneness.

In his book, The Miracle of Mindfulness, Zen Master, Thich Nhat Hanh states:

"Practice looking at all beings with the eyes of compassion: this is the meditation called the 'meditation on compassion.' The meditation on compassion must be realized during the hours you sit and during every moment you carry out service for others. No matter where you go or where you sit, remember the sacred call: 'Look at all beings with the eyes of compassion.'...We need to light our own torch in order to carry on. But the life of each one of us is connected with the life of those around us." (p. 59-60)

Compassion is optimum communication through Divine Inspiration. Compassion is different than sympathy because with sympathy there exists the inherent subtle energy that we feel sorry for someone. When we feel sorry for someone, we are not accepting them as an equal. Compassion involves the energy of equality and kindness. It allows us on some level to become the other person in order to assist them in the most optimum way. Compassion involves pure and selfless love, and we can achieve this in our Reiki practice through awareness, constant practice, and teachings from a real, touching Master in our lives. Reiki is only possible when a compassionate Master shares their energy in presence. It is the I-Thou.

When a Reiki Practitioner moves beyond awareness of self, or achieves the state of ego-less-ness, they arrive at this level of non-discrimination beyond conscious separation. I call this state of be-ing the "Unisonium," the state of oneness in harmony. This is the optimum healing state. How does one achieve this state? It is the connection, the linking, of the High Heart and the Ajna center. The turquoise of the High Heart contains the color of gold (as does the stone of turquoise). The gold in of the High Heart blends with the indigo-violet of the Ajna (Third Eye) Center to create ultraviolet. The ultraviolet energy births the channel through the Soul Star Center to the gold of the Tao Center. Ultraviolet is just beyond violet in the visible spectrum. Edgar Cayce advocated that the "Violet Ray" machine based on work by Tesla be used for healing. (You may still purchase this wonderful instrument through the Heritage Store of Virginia Beach, Virginia: 1-800-862-2923. Item #VRM, cost is approximately $190.00) The energy for the creation of ultraviolet in the healing field is the energy of Compassion. I have had many people tell me of the awakening of the High Heart Center. The High Heart does not open until the aspirant is spiritually ready. At some time after Reiki Level One, this Center of the High Heart begins to open. Many describe the initial process as a pain in the upper chest area, or as a feeling much like a "sore throat" that is much too low to be a sore throat. After this Center opens, there are many changes in self perception and dramatic life changes occur. It may become difficult, if not impossible, to eat meat, to judge people for their differences, and to be involved in any sort of negative energy exchange. This is the sacred Alchemy of the Spirit, the ultimate idealization of creating gold from lesser materials. In this analogy, then, the gold within the High Heart is activated or actualized. It is then possible for one to create the optimum field of healing. All 88,000 Chakras are harmonized. All Sacred Bodies are integrated. The Tao Center translates Compassion into harmony and powerful healing energy. Study the diagram of the Unisonium below, and note the dynamic level of higher achieved connection between Practitioner and Healee.

HIGH VIBRATION RESONANCE

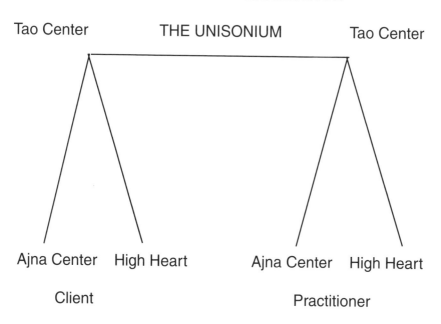

Tao Center   THE UNISONIUM   Tao Center

Ajna Center   High Heart   Ajna Center   High Heart

Client   Practitioner

I sense the colors of the Ajna and High Heart Centers as an ever-increasing shade of ultraviolet as this energy of compassion reaches the gold of the Tao center. Practitioner and Healee meet at this higher healing and vibrational level as they "observe noble silence" within. The field of energy of creative oneness is established and this high vibration should be maintained as long as is possible. You are closer to Light and self love.

HAND POSITION TECHNIQUE: OPENING THE GATE TO COMPASSION

Complete all other hand placements up to and including the Heart Center. You should be on the left side of the client. Leave your right hand upon the client's High Heart Center and gently slide your left hand beneath their left hand. Bring their left hand up to and near your own Heart Center, grasping their hand firmly yet gently. Hold this position as long as necessary or comfortable for you both. You may choose to add healing words, visualizations, or any of the Kotama Scripts (provided later).

POWER TECHNIQUE FOR ACCESS TO THE UNISONIUM

Practitioner: Begin with appropriate symbols above the client's Crown Center. Place hands on Crown Center position. Move into the "Gate of Compassion" by holding the Crown Center with the left hand while drawing the appropriate symbol above High Heart with the right hand (if you are right-handed). Or you may draw or visualize the symbol with your Third Eye or any other method that is effective for you. Place the right hand on the High Heart and move to the left side of the client. Gently lift the left hand with your left hand and hold the gateway position as long as is necessary.

Ask the client to take three long, deep breaths. As they inhale, ask them to breathe in blue, healing energy. As they exhale, ask them to breathe out old, stale, or tired energy. Then ask them to breathe in, relaxed and peaceful, blue healing energy and as they breathe out, exhale peace and Light. Soon they are surrounded and protected by peace and Light.

Practitioner: Breathe in unison with the client while holding the microcosmic orbit. Visualize that with every breath in, you are stepping up a golden step. There are eleven (11) sacred, golden steps. Each step symbolizes a major axis chakra in the Interdimensional system: 1) Root, 2) Sacral, 3) Solar Plexus, 4) Leydes, 5) Heart, 6) High Heart, 7) Throat, 8) Ajna, 9) Crown, 10) Soul Star, 11) Tao. At the Tao you become one. You may actually choose first to breathe into each chakra and exhale from each chakra, then ascend the sacred steps with another eleven breaths.

THE UNISONIUM SELF-HEALING MEDITATION

It might prove beneficial to first practice the technique of achieving the Unisonium through self-healing applications before actually working with a client. Through practice, you are able to integrate with and feel the gradual escalation of vital internal energy and adjust your breathing pattern according to your comfort level. If, at any time in your practice you feel light-headed, discontinue the practice, and breathe normally and naturally.

Sit in a comfortable position. Close your eyes and take a deep, cleansing breath. Press your tongue to the roof of your mouth just behind the hard palate. (This creates the "inner smile" of tranquility and awareness.) Affirm to yourself, "I am in harmony with the Universe." Contract the muscles of the pelvic floor by tensing the buttock muscles. (Some call such a contraction a "Kegel") You must maintain the attention at both sites throughout the practice, as they are the "switches" to complete the flow of energy current within the microcosmic orbit. Affirm to yourself, "I am a vessel for Universal Energy." (If the mirror image of the Mental Symbol is drawn next to itself it appears to be the reflection of an ornate vase or vessel.) Breathe in deeply, all the way to your Root Center, filling your entire body with yellow radiating energy like the fire of the Solar Plexus Center. Breathe in that radiating energy into each of the following chakras: Sacral, Solar Plexus, Leydes, Heart, High Heart, Throat, Ajna, Crown, Soul Star, and Tao. You may include hand placements as you breathe in and out of each of these Centers. At the Soul Star and Tao Centers, place your hands on the High Heart (L.H.) and Ajna Centers (R.H.) As you breathe into the the Tao Center, draw down the fine gold energy around you with the next breath, and breathe it into the root center. (Begin hand placements again at the Root Center.) Then breathe gold from the Tao Center through the root up into each of the following and hold your breath for about three seconds: (the Root), Sacral, Solar Plexus, Leydes, Heart, High Heart, Throat, Ajna, Crown, Tao, and back again to the Root. I suggest that you begin the first week with a set of three cycles through the chakras, and add one more cycle each week or so until you reach twelve or twenty-one. This meditation increases energy, vitality, and longevity if practiced daily. When your practice is complete, sweep your aura three times.

There are many other methods to practice the microcosmic orbit meditation. I suggest that you read books by Mantak Chia for further information, including the advanced techniques of "Immortal Breathing."

MEDITATION ON TWIN HEARTS

The following meditation is reprinted with permission from Pranic Healing, by Choa Kok Sui, published by Samuel Weiser Publishing.

"Without leaving the house, one may know all there is in heaven and earth. Without peeping from the window, one may see the ways of heaven. Those who go out learn less and less the more they travel. Wherefore does the sage know all without going anywhere, see all without looking, do nothing and yet achieve (the Goal) !"
Lao Tsu, Tao Te Ching

"THE ILLUMINATION TECHNIQUE, or 'Meditation on the Twin Hearts,' is a technique to achieve Buddhic consciousness or cosmic consciousness or illumination. It is also a form of service to the world because the world is harmonized to a certain degree by blessing the entire earth with loving kindness.

'Meditation on the Twin Hearts' is based on the principle that some of the major chakras are entry points or gateways to certain levels or horizons of consciousness. To achieve illumination or Buddhic consciousness, it is necessary to fully activate the crown chakra. The crown chakra, when fully activated, becomes like a cup. To be more exact, the twelve inner petals open and turn upward like a cup to receive spiritual energies which are distributed to other parts of the body. The crowns worn by kings and queens are but poor physical replicas or symbols of the indescribably resplendent crown chakra of a fully developed person. The fully activated crown chakra is symbolized as the Holy Grail.

The crown chakra can only be fully activated when the heart

chakra is first fully activated. The heart chakra is a replica of the crown chakra. When you look at the heart chakra, it looks like the inner chakra of the crown chakra, which has twelve golden petals. The heart chakra is the lower correspondence of the crown chakra. The crown chakra is the center of illumination and divine love or oneness with all. To explain what is divine love and illumination to an ordinary person is just like trying to explain what color is to a blind man. The heart chakra is the center of higher emotions. It is the center for compassion, joy, affection, consideration, mercy and other refined emotions. Without developing higher refined emotions, how can one possibly experience divine love?

There are many ways of activating the heart and crown chakras. You can use physical movements, hatha yoga, yogic breathing techniques, mantras or words of power, and visualization techniques. All of these techniques are effective but are not fast enough. One of the most effective and fastest ways to activate these chakras is to do meditation on loving kindness or to bless the whole earth with loving kindness. By using the heart chakra and the crown chakra in blessing the earth with loving-kindness, they become channels for spiritual energies; thereby becoming activated in the process. By blessing the earth with loving kindness, you are doing a form of world service. And by blessing the earth with loving-kindness, you are in turn blessed many times. It is in blessing that you are blessed. It is in giving that you receive. That is the law!

A person with a fully activated crown chakra does not necessarily achieve illumination for he or she has yet to learn how to make use of the crown chakra to achieve illumination. It is just like having a sophisticated computer but not knowing how to operate it. Once the crown chakra has been fully activated, then you have to do meditation on the light, on the mantra Aum, and on the gap between the two Aums. Intense concentration should be focused not only on the mantra Aum but especially on the gap between the two Aums. It is by fully and intensely concentrating on the light and the gap between the two Aums that illumination, or samadhi, is achieved!

With most people, their other chakras are quite activated. The basic chakra, sex chakra, and solar plexus chakra are activated in practically all people. With these people, their instincts for self survival, sex drive and their tendency to react with their lower emotions are very active. With the persuasiveness of modern education and work that requires the use of the mental faculty, the ajna chakra and the throat chakra are developed in a lot of people. What is not developed in most people are the heart and crown chakra. Modern education, unfortunately, tends to overemphasize the development of the throat chakra and the ajna chakra or the development of the concrete mind and the abstract mind. The development of the heart has been neglected. Because of this, you may encounter people who are quite intelligent but very abrasive. This type of person has not yet matured emotionally or the heart chakra is quite underdeveloped. Though he or she is intelligent and may be successful, human relationships are very poor, with hardly any friends and no family or a broken family. By using the 'Meditation On the Twin Hearts,' a person becomes harmoniously balanced.

Whether the abstract and concrete mind will be used constructively or destructively depends upon the development of the heart. When the solar plexus chakra is overdeveloped and the heart chakra is underdeveloped, or when the lower emotions are active and the higher emotions are underdeveloped, then the mind would probably be used destructively. Without the development of the heart in most people, world peace will be an unattainable dream. This is why the development of the heart should be emphasized in the educational system.

People less than 18 years old should not practice the illumination techniques since the body cannot yet withstand too much subtle energy. This may even manifest as physical paralysis in the long run. People with heart ailments should not practice 'Meditation on the Twin Hearts' since it may result in severe pranic heart congestion. It is important that people who intend to practice 'Meditation On the Twin Hearts' regularly should also practice self-purification or character building through daily inner reflection. 'Meditation On the Twin Hearts' not only activates the heart chakra and the crown chakra but also the other chakras. Because of this, both the positive and negative characteristics of the practitioner will be magnified or activated. This can easily be verified by the practitioner himself and through clairvoyant observation.

PROCEDURE

1) Cleansing the etheric body through physical exercise: Do physical exercise for about five minutes. Doing physical exercise has a cleansing and energizing effect on the etheric body. Light grayish matter or used up prana is expelled from the etheric body when exercising. Physical exercises have to be done to minimize possible pranic congestion since this meditation generates a lot of subtle energies in the etheric body.

2) Invocation for divine blessing: Invoking the blessing of one's Spiritual Guides is very important. Each spiritual aspirant has spiritual guides, whether he or she is consciously aware of them or not. The invocation is required for one's protection, help and guidance. Without making the invocation, practicing any advanced meditational technique could be dangerous You can make your own invocation. I usually use this invocation: 'Father, I humbly invoke Thy divine blessing for protection, guidance, help and illumination! With thanks and in full faith!'

3) Activating the heart chakra and blessing the entire earth with loving-kindness: Press your front heart chakra with your finger for a few seconds. This is to make concentration on the front heart chakra easier. Concentrate on the front heart chakra and bless the earth with loving kindness. You may improvise your own blessing with loving kindness. I usually use this blessing:

Blessing the Earth with Loving Kindness

From the Heart of God,
Let the entire earth be blessed with loving kindness.
Let the entire earth be blessed with great joy, happiness and divine peace.
Let the entire earth be blessed with understanding, harmony, good will and will to good. So be it!

From the Heart of God,
Let the hearts of all sentient beings be filled with divine love and kindness.
Let the hearts of all sentient beings be filled with great joy, happiness and divine peace.
Let the hearts of all sentient beings be filled with understanding, harmony, good will and will-to-good. With thanks, so be it!

For beginners this blessing is done only once or twice. Do not overdo this blessing at the start. Some may even feel a slight pranic congestion around the heart area. This is because your etheric body is not sufficiently clean. Apply localized sweeping to remove the congestion.

This blessing should not be done mechanically. You should feel and fully appreciate the implications in each phrase. You may also use visualization. When blessing the earth with loving kindness, visualize the aura of the earth as becoming dazzling pink. When blessing the earth with great joy, happiness and peace, visualize people with heavy difficult problems smiling and their hearts filled with joy, faith, hope and peace. Visualize their problems becoming lighter and their faces lightening up. When blessing the earth with harmony, good will and will to good, visualize people or nations on the verge of fighting or fighting each other reconciling. Visualize these people putting down their arms and embracing each other. Visualize them being filled with good intentions and filled with the will to carry out this good intention. This blessing can be directed to a nation or nations, a family or a person or a group of persons. Do not direct this blessing on a specific infant or specific children because they might be overwhelmed by the intense energy generated by the meditation.

4) Activating the crown chakra and blessing the earth with loving kindness: Press the crown with your finger for several seconds to facilitate concentration on the crown chakra and bless the entire earth with loving kindness. When the crown chakra is fully opened, some of you will feel something blooming on top of the head and some will also feel something pressing on the crown. After the crown chakra has been activated, concentrate simultaneously on the crown chakra and the heart chakra, and bless the earth with loving kindness several times. This will align the heart chakra and the crown chakra, thereby making the blessing much more potent.

5) To achieve illumination and meditation on the light, on the Aum and the gap between the two Aums: Visualize a grain of dazzling white light on the crown or at the center inside the head, and simultaneously mentally utter the mantra, Aum. Concentrate intensely on the point of light, on the Aum and on the gap between the two Aums. When mentally uttering the mantra Aum, you will notice that the Aums are not continuous and that there is a slight gap between two mantras or between

two Aums. Do this meditation for five to ten minutes. When the spiritual aspirant can fully concentrate simultaneously on the point of light and on the gap between the two Aums, he or she will experience an 'inner explosion of light'. The entire being will be filled with light! He or she will have the first glimpse of illumination and the first experience of divine ecstasy! To experience Buddhic consciousness or illumination is to experience and understand what Jesus meant when he said: "If thine eye be single, the whole body shall he full of light." (Luke 11: 34) . "For behold, the kingdom of heaven is within you." (Luke 17:21).

For some people, it may take years before they experience an initial glimpse of illumination or Buddhic consciousness. Others may take months while others may take weeks. For the very few, they achieve initial expansion of consciousness on the first try. This is usually done with the help from an elder or a facilitator.

When doing this meditation, the aspirant should be neutral. He or she should not be obsessed with results or filled with too many expectations. Otherwise, he or she will be actually meditating on the expectations or the expected results rather than on the point of light, the Aum and the gap between the two Aums.

6) Releasing excess energy: After the end of the meditation, the excess energy should be released by blessing the earth with Light, Love and Peace. Otherwise, the etheric body will become congested and the visible body will deteriorate in the long run because of too much energy. Other esoteric schools release the excess energy by visualizing the chakras projecting out the excess energy and the chakras becoming smaller and dimmer, but this approach does not put the excess energy into constructive use.

7) Giving thanks: After the end of the meditation, always give thanks to your spiritual guides for the divine blessing.

8) Strengthening the visible physical body through massage and more physical exercises After the end of the meditation, massage your body and do physical exercise for about five minutes. The purpose is to further cleanse and strengthen the visible body since more used-up prana is expelled out of the body. This facilitates the assimilation of the pranic and spiritual energies, thereby enhancing the beauty and health of the practitioner. Massaging and exercising after this meditation also reduces the possibility of pranic congestion or energy getting in certain parts of the body which may lead to illness. You can also gradually cure yourself of some ailments by doing exercises after doing the 'Meditation On the Twin Hearts'. It is very important to exercise after the meditation, otherwise, the visible physical body will inevitably he weakened. Although the etheric body will become very bright and strong, the visible physical body will become weak because it will not be able to withstand the leftover energy generated by the meditation in the long run. You have to experience it yourself to fully appreciate what I am saying.

Some of you have the tendency not to do physical exercise after this meditation but to continue savoring the blissful state. This tendency should be overcome, otherwise your physical health will deteriorate in the long run.

Sometimes when a spiritual aspirant meditates, he or she may experience unusual physical movements for a limited period of time. This is quite normal since the etheric channels are being cleansed.

The instructions may seem quite long but the meditation is short, simple and very effective! It requires only ten to fifteen minutes excluding the time required for the physical exercises.

There are many degrees of illumination. The art of 'intuiting' or 'direct synthetic knowing' requires constant practice (meditation) for a long duration of time. To be more exact, it requires many incarnations to develop facility in the use of this Buddhic faculty.

Blessing the earth with loving-kindness can be done in group as a form of world service. When done in a group for this purpose, first bless the earth with loving-kindness through the heart chakra, then through the crown chakra, then through both the crown chakra and the heart chakra. Release the excess energy after the end of the meditation. The other parts of the meditation are omitted. The blessing can be directed, not only to the entire earth, but also to a specific nation or group of nations. The potency of the blessing is increased many times when done in group. For example, when the blessing is done by a group of seven, the effect or potency is equal to more than one hundred people doing it separately.

Just as pranic healing can miraculously cure simple and severe ailments, the 'Meditation on Twin Hearts' when practiced by a large number of people can also miraculously heal the entire earth. This message is directed to readers with sufficient maturity and the will-to-good.

MEDITATION ON THE TWIN HEARTS

1) Clean the etheric body, do physical exercise for about five minutes.

2) Invoke for divine blessing.

3) Activate the heart chakra, concentrate on it, and bless the entire earth with loving-kindness.

4) Activate the crown chakra, concentrate on it, and bless the entire earth with loving kindness. Then bless the earth with loving kindness simultaneously through the crown chakra and the heart chakra.

5) To achieve illumination, concentrate on the point of light on the Aum, and on the gap between the two Aums.

6) To release excess energy, bless the earth with light, love and peace.

7) Give thanks.

8) To strengthen the visible physical body; massage face and body, and do physical exercise for about five minutes.

   'Meditation on the Twin Hearts' is a very powerful tool in bringing about world peace; therefore, this meditational technique should be disseminated. Permission is granted to all interested persons to reprint, recopy and reproduce the 'Meditation on the Twin Hearts' with proper acknowledgment to both author and publisher.

   Note: Aum is a Sanskrit word for the Supreme Being; in Arabic, Allah; in Chinese, Tao; and in English, God."
Gratitude to Master Choa Kok Sui

In his book, How To Know Higher Worlds, Rudolph Steiner relates:

"We must develop forbearance (or tolerance) toward other people, other beings, and events. We must suppress all unnecessary criticism of imperfection, evil, and wickedness and seek rather to understand everything that comes to meet us. Just as the sun does not withdraw its light from wickedness and evil, so we, too, should not withdraw our understanding and sympathy from anyone. When we meet adversity, we should not indulge in negative judgments but accept the inevitable and try, as best we can, to turn it to the good. Similarly, instead of considering the opinions of others only from our own standpoint, we should try to put ourselves into their position." (p. 121)

Steiner believes that we develop higher "organs" that assist us to "perceive living and autonomous beings that belong to a world very different from the world of the physical senses." "The twelve-petalled lotus (near the heart) is formed in the following way. First, we pay attention to directing the sequence of our thoughts--this so-called 'practice of the control of thoughts.' Just as thinking and true and meaningful thoughts develops the sixteen-petalled lotus flower, so inwardly controlling our thinking processes develops the twelve-petalled flower." (Ibid. p. 120) This is the Anahata Center.

This form of "mindfulness" leads to the cultivation of a deeper level of spiritual understanding:

"It then becomes clear that we are part of a higher spiritual context, which determines our qualities, and our destiny. We begin to understand the law of human life, namely karma. We realize that our lower self, which shapes our existence in the present, is only one of the many forms our higher being can assume. And in this way we realize that it is possible to work on the lower self from the perspective of the higher self in order to be-come more and more perfect...by reaching this stage of inner development, students of the spirit actually become new beings." (Ibid. p. 149-149)

This evolution, the be-coming of "new beings" is not so dif-ferent from the evolution of one of Buddha's followers, Kuan Yin, who first began life as a man, but changed gender in order to balance the Yin/Yang energies.

TECHNIQUE: BALANCING THE CHAKRAS THROUGH THE HIGH HEART

You may be familiar with the more traditional chakra bal-ancing technique that utilizes a system like the Menorah, the seven-branched candelabrum symbolizing the seven days of creation. In this technique, you place one hand upon the Crown Center (7), the other on, near, or above the Root Center (1). From (7), you move to the Ajna (6), while the other hand moves from (1) to (2), the Sacral Center. From (6) you move to the (5) Throat Center, while (2) moves to (3) the Solar Plexus. (If a person has been abused physically or verbally, this balance position is most beneficial.) (5) and (3) merge at the Heart Center (4).

For the High Heart Balance, you begin on the left side of your client. Place your right hand on the Ajna Center and your left hand on the High Heart. Visualize that you are moving into the Unisonium as you breathe in harmony with your client and utilize the Microcosmic Orbit. Draw golden light from the Tao Center down into the client's Ajna and the High Heart. Hold this position for five or more minutes. All chakras are balanced in this manner, but if you choose, you may also move from the High Heart Balance into the traditional balancing technique listed above.

BALANCING THE SPIRITUAL BODY

The Inner Triangle Balance

PRACTITIONER STANDS, CLIENT IS SEATED ON A NON-METAL CHAIR.

Practitioner places left hand on the high heart center, right hand on back between shoulder blades, directly across from left hand. Hold for three minutes. I play the background music of "The Eternal OM" or "Golden Bowls." (Optional: both chant "OM" aloud (or silently) quietly together and breathe in unison free of background music. Practitioner may choose to chant "OM" to self if you feel that client would be hesitant to participate.)

Pause chanting and breathe normally, preparing for next position: practitioner moves right hand from the middle of the back to the left shoulder blade at high center. Hold for three minutes while chanting or meditating to music. Breathe normally as you move hand to next position, right shoulder blade at high center. Hold for three minutes, chanting the "OM" or meditating to music. Breathe normally. Move right hand to crown. Hold for three minutes, chanting or meditating. Sweep upper body front and back, including crown, three times.

The Inner Triangle is completed with the High Heart Center as it is surrounded by the creation of the second energy of the Crown Center Triangle. You may also choose to utilize color in this balance, utilizing the color Turquoise (with gold) for the Inner Triangle, and Violet for the completion of the Crown Center Triangle.

INNER TRIANGLE BALANCE

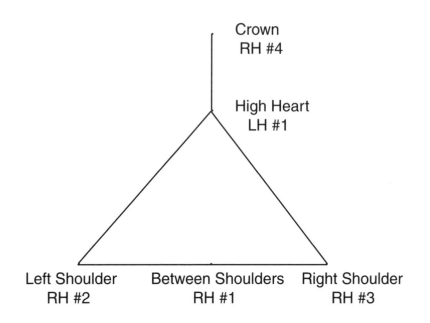

Crown
RH #4

High Heart
LH #1

Left Shoulder   Between Shoulders   Right Shoulder
RH #2   RH #1   RH #3

MENDING AND INTEGRATING
THE MENTAL BODY GRID

YOU MAY UTILIZE THIS TECHNIQUE FOR SELF HEALING, ABSEN-
TIA HEALING, OR YOU MAY GUIDE YOUR CLIENT THROUGH THE PRO-
CESS.

In meditation I was given the following potential process for
mending the mental body grid:

I was channeling energy for a person with Anorexia Nervosa.
I always felt that the Mental Body is present within the consciousness of each cell, not just in the area of the brain. I saw
the body of this individual as surrounded by tiny dimensional
triangles (three-sided pyramids). They were different luminous
colors, depending upon which part of the body system (chakras)
they were connected to. The apex of each thin pyramid was
attached to the nucleus within each cell of the body. I noticed

that in this case, some of the pyramids were eroded, and where they were eroded, they were dark, dull, and life-less. Most of the erosion was around the Solar Plexus, Sacral, and Throat areas. There was also some erosion around the left side of the head near the temple.

I asked my Guide how I might serve as the Highest Channel to assist in any potential healing of this grid work. I felt as though the healing was most needed in "Right Thinking." In other words, rejection of self, lack of forgiveness of self or others, or the acceptance of other people's negative thoughts or opinions had created the milieu for this opportunistic decay of the Mental Body Grid. (I am aware that all healing is self healing, especially in such a case.) This particular dis-ease also seemed very karmic in nature, as it appeared to be an extreme control issue based upon punishment of self.

I saw the symbol for Universal Consciousness/ the Mental Symbol. Then I saw a huge, golden pyramid connected at the Apex to the nucleus of what I perceived of as Universal Mind. I asked the individual's guide to connect each eroded pyramid to the apex of the Universal Mind Construct. (Leaving all in Divine Order for the Highest Good.) The darkness began to lift bit by bit in each of the areas involved in the healing process. There seemed to be a bit of color difference, indicating yet weakness, but I felt that perhaps a new paradigm was in process. I was very aware that the individual had not yet decided to integrate this new "thought form" energy, as it seemed to be yet unstable. I feel that all healing, as self healing is part of a soul's choice. In three days, I felt that the energy will be accepted and integrated, or rejected by the individual. I also asked that any energy or negative thought forms that were not serving this individual's Highest Good also be released. (In Divine Order.)

I thanked the Guides and all involved in this process.

"When someone asks what there is to do, light the candle in his hand."
Rumi

THE ANCIENT CHRISTIAN TEXTS

The ancient mystery writings of the Christian tradition reflect the fact that Jesus and his followers were involved in healing as connected to the energy of life as in The Essene Gospel of Peace Book Three, Lost Scrolls of the Essene Brotherhood, by Edmond Szekely:

The Angel of Life

"Seek not the law in thy scriptures, for the law is
          Life,
Whereas the scriptures are only words...
In everything that is life the law is written.
It is found in the grass, in the trees,
In the river, in the mountains, in the birds of heaven,
In the forest creatures and the fishes of the sea;
But it is found chiefly in thyselves.
All living things are nearer to God
Than the scriptures which are without life.
God so made life and all living things...
God wrote not the law in the pages of books,
But in thy heart and in thy spirit.
They are in thy breath, thy blood, thy bone;
In thy flesh, thine eyes, thine ears,
And in every little part of thy body. (p.35)

These "Lost Scrolls" of the original Hebrew and Aramic tests also translated the text of the "Angel of Eternal Life":

The Angel of Eternal Life

"...The first follower of the Law was Enoch,
The first of the healers, of the wise,
The happy, the glorious, the strong,
Who drove back sickness and drove back death.
He did obtain a source of remedies
To withstand sickness and to withstand death;
To withstand the evil and infection
Which ignorance of the Law
Had created against the bodies of mortals.
We invoke Enoch,
The master of Life,
The Founder of our Brotherhood,
The man of the Law,
The wisest of all beings...
To all the Children of Light
He gave the good things of life:
He was the first bearer of the Law." (p. 55)

And "The Holy Law":
The Holy Law

"Thou, O Holy Law,
The tree of Life
That standeth in the middle
Of the Eternal Sea,
That is called,
The Tree of Healing,
The Tree of Powerful Healing,
The Tree of all Healing,
And upon which rests the seeds
Of all we invoke." (p. 73)

In <u>The Secret Teachings of Jesus, the Four Gnostic Gospels,</u> the book of Thomas explains:

"Whoever finds the interpretation of these sayings will not taste death." Jesus said, "If your leaders say to you, 'Behold the kingdom is in the sky,' then the birds in the sky will get there before you. If they say to you, 'it is in the sea,' then the fish will get there before you. Rather, the kingdom is inside you and outside you. When you know yourselves, then you will be known, and will understand that you are children of the living Father. But if you do not know yourselves, then you live in poverty, and embody poverty...for there are five trees in Paradise for you. They do not change, summer, or winter, and their leaves do not drop. Whoever knows about them will not taste death." (p. 20-23)

In another passage of the book of Thomas, Jesus explains where we come from:

"If some say to you, 'Where have you come from?' say to them, 'We have come from the light, where the light came into being by itself, established itself, and appeared in an image of light. If they say to you, 'Are you the light?' say, 'We are its children, and we are the chosen of the living Father.' If they ask you, 'What is the evidence of your Father in you?' tell them, 'It is motion and rest.'"
(p. 28)

The <u>Secret Teachings</u> are translations of the "Nag Hammadi" texts which were found at the base of the cliffs near the Nile River of Upper Egypt:

"Most of the texts reflect a mystical, esoteric religious movement that we term Gnosticism, from the word gnosis, 'knowledge...' They searched for a higher knowledge, a more profound insight into the deep and secret things of God. Like other mystics, Gnostics admitted that this saving knowledge cannot be acquired through the memorization of phrases or the study of books; nevertheless, like other mystics, they composed numerous documents explaining the nature of spiritual gnosis. Such Gnostic texts proclaim a completely good and transcendent God, whose enlightened greatness is utterly unfathomable and essential indescribable. Yet the divine Other can be experienced in a person's inner life, for the spirit within is actually the divine self, the inner spark or ray of heavenly light. The tragedy of human existence, however, is that most people fail to realize the fulfillment of the divine life, because of the harsh world that functions as the stage for the human drama...Transformation, Gnostics maintained, is accomplished through a call from God--the God without and within--to discover true knowledge and rest. For Gnostic Christians, the source of the divine call is Christ." (<u>The Secret Teachings of Jesus,</u> p. xvi.)

The four texts of the "Nag Hammadi" were based upon secret teachings of his followers James, his brother, Judas Thomas, regarded as the twin brother of Jesus, and the spiritual disciple, John. James begins, "Since you have asked me to send you a secret book revealed to me and Peter by the Lord, I could not refuse you." The Gospel of Thomas begins, "These are the secret sayings that the living Jesus spoke and Judas Thomas, the Twin recorded." The Book of Thomas begins, "The secret sayings that the Savior spoke to Judas Thomas and that I, Matthew, recorded as I was walking and listening to them speak with each other." And the Secret Book of John begins, "The teaching of the Savior, and the revelation of the mysteries and things hidden in silence, things that he taught to his disciple John." These "secret texts" held information that was rejected or believed to be too confidential or controversial for the general public. They were discovered in their hiding place in 1945, and much has been done since that time to suppress or discredit the information held in these texts as they contradict the (Council of Nicea altered) texts of the New Testament. And why were they hidden? Were they hidden to protect the knowledge in and of the secret teachings, or hidden to protect them from destruction by those in power at the time? A scholar of these texts revealed her viewpoint that she believed that Jesus was scorned and mistreated most of his life for one belief: that God lived in each of us, (dwelled within rather than without) and because of that, each of us had direct access to God. That one precept was in direct conflict with the religious power structure of that time. She also felt that Jesus considered Himself to be a failure as He failed to convince the Jews that He was the son of God (and that we all are). I had heard it said that there are truly only two "religions," one that believes that God is in us and the other that believes that God is (exists) elsewhere. There is also controversy concerning the celibacy, the crucifixion, and the resurrection of Jesus. Another controversy is the source of His healing power. Some ancient sutras (writings) mention a St. Isa (Jesus?) who came to Tibet. He spent years studying the mysteries there. Were one of those mysteries the ancient hands-on healing art that we know now as Reiki?

Why does so much controversy surround the individual known as Jesus? I believe the answer to that is because Jesus taught in parables and became a mirror to people's understanding. So, in effect, He may have appeared quite different to each person who encountered Him. He became to each the teacher/spiritual leader that they most needed to enlighten (in-Light-en) them. In The Secret Teachings of Jesus, Jesus asks his disciples, "...tell me whom I am like." "Simon Peter said to Him, 'You are like a just angel.' Matthew said to Him, 'You are like a wise philosopher.' Thomas said to him, 'Teacher my mouth is utterly unable to say whom you are like.' Jesus said, 'I am not your teacher. And he took Thomas and withdrew, and told him three things.'"(p. 21) Later Jesus states, "A prophet is not popular in the home town, a doctor does not heal family and friends." (p.25) (I mention this passage in particular for all who do Reiki who find that their family and friends are less than receptive to their great gift.) Over and over again, Jesus' disciples desired his wisdom, but continuously he taught in parables. This is very closely related to one of the ancient master-teacher methods of instruction known as Nien ghud Tibetan mystical masters. Was He avoiding the "right" answer to their questions because He did not wish to create laws? I feel that He was attempting to lead them away from "knowledge" and into their hearts. It is, perhaps, the same age-old salvation question: is one saved by Faith or Works? And where does one place their faith, in wisdom (knowledge) or in actions? The true quest is to move away from knowledge and into the spirit. It is not what we know that counts, but rather who we are spiritually as a vessel of God. In his book <u>Mysticism Empowering the Spirit Within</u>, Hua-Ching Ni states:

> "A person can only link with the subtlety of universal spiritual reality by going through the same training as the ancient ones. Without this study, training or experience, a person's recognition or consciousness will be limited to the physical sphere of life and will not dip into the spiritual sphere...However, I must tell you that knowing the spiritual realm is not everything in life. It is just one part of a complete life.

> I must also tell you that knowing information about the spiritual realm is not as important as one's experience and facility in energy practice. Many times as a Chinese medicinal doctor, I met scholars or teachers who had developed a deep knowledge of Buddhist or Christian theology through study. However, when they suffered a stroke due to high blood pressure or another problem, their minds became blocked and they did not have access to this intellectual knowledge. They told me, 'This knowledge helped me earn a living, but it did not last when my mind no longer existed. Nothing I had learned from books helped the reality of my illness.' Please understand from this that knowledge about the spiritual realm is only on an intellectual level; the practice and realistic development is what is most important. Talking about God is not the same as reaching God." [11]

---

11. Hua-Ching Ni, <u>Mysticism, Empowering the Spirit Within</u>, The Shrine of the Breath of the Eternal Tao, Malibu, CA, 1992, p. 159.

SOUL'S LABYRINTH
THE SPIRAL JOURNEY

You may take this journey on seven levels. The first level begins with the physical. Create a large spiral in your yard like the one illustrated. With a partner as your physical guide, you are blindfolded. Begin at point "A", which represents your current age. With assistance from your physical and spiritual guides, you begin your journey back through time, back through your life. You walk slowly until you feel the need to stop. (Your partner marks this place with a stone.) When you stop, your physical partner will ask you the following questions:

1.) <u>How old are you here?</u> (Meaning the time of your life where you have stopped.)

2.) <u>What emotion has stopped you?</u> Or: <u>What do you feel here?</u>

3.) <u>Who is this emotion about?</u> Or: <u>Who or what caused this emotion in you?</u>

4.) <u>What color is this emotion?</u> (Pause for answer) <u>How big is this emotion?</u>

5.) <u>Where did you store this emotion in your body?</u> Or: <u>Which chakra is it stored in?</u>

6.) <u>Can you talk to the one who created this emotion in you in order to heal it?</u>

7.) <u>Can you release this emotion now?</u> Then: <u>Pick up the parts of soul fragments that you you lost.</u>

8.) <u>Is everything healed here?</u> If no is the answer, ask, "<u>What else do we need to do?</u>"

9.) If yes is the answer, ask, "<u>What do you need to affirm to yourself?</u>" (Silent or aloud)

10.)Then: "<u>Are you ready to go on?</u>" If yes:

Continue on your spiral path until you stop again. Ask the same questions, and then continue on. When you reach the end of the spiral, ask, "Is there anything with your birth that needs healed?" If the answer is yes, begin with the second option in question #2 and continue through to #9. Ask "Are we complete here?" Then ask them to come back through the spiral to their current age, repeating the following affirmation as they do so: "I am free of all limitation. I am free to love myself and others."

If space is limited, you may choose to take this Labyrinth Journey on a large piece of paper. Your partner should sit on the side of your non-dominant hand. Hold a pen or pencil in your non-dominant hand. Begin at point "A" on the paper, and work slowly back the spiral with your eyes closed. Your partner only exerts slight pressure on your hand only to direct your course. When you feel the need to stop, your partner will ask the questions above, and follow through the entire exercise. You may choose to include the **Ceremony of Birth Rite Tea** following the Labyrinth Exercise.

SOUL'S LABYRINTH, THE SPIRAL JOURNEY

Partner: Please mark each point on the next page at which the Journeyer stops. List the age, emotion, and chakra where energy was stored.

THE REVELATION OF THE LABYRINTH

In order to truly know who we are, we must first remove the layers of dust from our soul. We may find in doing so that we have been playing roles so well throughout our lives that we have lost our true identity. It is buried somewhere in the es-

SOUL'S LABYRINTH

sence and history of our past. We may live our lives motivated by forces deep within us--in our own personal labyrinth--that we have long forgotten. We can choose to be trapped within that labyrinth, or find the way to release ourselves from the pain, trauma, or fear of past events that contributed to the creation of this labyrinth. Joseph Campbell writes of such deep forces within us: "C.G. Jung, for example, identifies two fundamentally different systems of unconsciously motivated response in the human being. One he terms the personal unconscious. It is based on a context of forgotten, neglected, or suppressed memory images derived from personal experience (infantile impressions, shocks, frustrations, satisfactions, etc.), such as Freud recognized and analyzed in his therapy. The other he calls the collective unconscious. Its contents--which he calls archetypes--are just such images. No one has yet been able to tell us how it got there; but there it is!" Campbell also relates how the image of the labyrinth has long been a part of the history and mystery schools of many cultures:

"In archaic art, the labyrinth--home of the child-consuming Minotaur--was represented in the figure of a spiral. The spiral also appears spontaneously in certain stages of meditation, as well as to people going to sleep under ether. It is a prominent device, furthermore, at the silent entrances and within the dark passages of the ancient Irish kingly burial ground of New Grange. These facts suggest that a constellation of images, denoting the plunge and dissolution of consciousness in the darkness of non-being must have been employed intentionally, from an early date, to represent the analogy of threshold rites to the mystery of the entry of the child into the womb for birth. And this suggestion is reinforced by the further fact that the paleolithic caves of Southern France and northern Spain, which are now dated by most authorities circa 30,000-10,000 B.C., were certain sanctuaries...where darkness no longer is an absence of light, but an experienced force."[12]

---

12. Joseph Campbell, Primitive Mythology, the Masks of God, Penguin Books, NewYork, New York, 1959 (Viking Press), p. 65-66

Campbell also writes:

> "The labyrinth, maze, and spiral were associated in ancient Crete and Babylon with the internal organs of the human anatomy as well as with the underworld, the one being a microcosm of the other. The object of the tomb-builder would have been to make the tomb as much like the body of the mother as he was able, since to enter the next world, the spirit would have to be reborn."[13]

Most ancient mystery schools were based upon the notion of death and rebirth. The individual survived a ritual that simulated death in order to be born to a new life. In Shamanism, this is referred to as experiencing the "Shaman's Death".

Allow yourself to experience this Labyrinth Exercise free of expectation and fear. Let the process unfold without analyzing or processing your answers. Just let your subconscious mind or your Higher Self be your guide. Feel what you need to feel!

PART TWO:
AFFIRMATION OF COMPLETION OF LABYRINTH
Kotama: The Power of the Spoken Word

Affirmations are only as powerful as the energy and intention behind them. Unless there is energy, there can be little power for manifestation. For power to invoke our spoken word, it is essential to move into the higher energy field of the Unisonium. There you can tune into Spirit and your Higher Consciousness (Higher Self) and in **Divine Order, for the Highest Good** create the space in the universe for the power of KOTAMA, the word. However, you must link to a Higher Consciousness or ask for Divine Assistance from the Light (or whatever is your personal Source of Power, Life, and Light). You may, in a similar manner, manifest with with Divine Thought or Divine Image (Visualization).

How is this process different from prayer? It is different in

---

13. Ibid, p. 69

this way: With prayer, most people ask an outside source (God or Angels) to make something happen for them without any other effort on their part. I have heard this concept or use of God as being limited to "the Great Wish Vending Machine in the Sky." With Kotama, we merge with the Light Source to co-create. I do not intend to diminish the Power of Prayer in any way, as I know it is very powerful when used for Divine Order and to serve the Highest Good. Recently I heard a story of a woman who happened upon a bad car accident. She stopped her car and began to pray for a woman who had been seriously injured. The spirit of the woman for whom she was praying had left her body and witnessed this stranger's concern and prayer. She saw this woman link in her consciousness to a Higher Power, and then an Incredible Light came down from above through this stranger and was directed to the broken body of the accident victim. The spirit of the accident victim was drawn back into her body, and a Great Peace filled her soul and body. This "Near Death Experience" enlightened this woman to the potent power of self-less prayer. No one else remembered this anonymous woman of prayer even being present at the time. However, the spirit of the woman for whom she was praying had taken note of the license plate, and later contacted her to thank her for saving her life through prayer.

Kotama is like prayer in linking, free of fear, to Higher Consciousness. There can be no negative attachments to any emotion when the Invocation of the Word is practiced. Fear limits access to the Higher Planes. It is a karmic block. In the Tattvarthadhigama Sutra, it is written, "Right belief, right knowledge, right conduct--these together constitute the path to liberation." And later, the Sutra explains:

> "The soul, owing to its being with passion, assimilates matter which is fit to form karmas. This is bondage. The main divisions of the nature of karma are knowldege-obscuring, perception (darsana)-obscuring, feeling-karma, deluding, age-determining, body-making, family-determining, and obstructive. There is the maturing and fruition of karmas. After fruition the karmas fall off. Meritorious karmas are the pleasure-

bearing, good-age-producing, good-body-producing, and high-family-determining. The karmas other than these are demeritorious karmas."[3]

The key words are, "after fruition, the karmas fall off." In healing the "feeling-karma," we are advancing beyond, transcending, the limitation, the bondage, of past karma.

THE PROCESS OF INITIATION OF KOTAMA

You may duplicate the Invocation for the Initiation of Kotama listed on the next page. You may write upon the back side of that paper your "Word" or that which you wish to bring into fruition. Fold the paper into three triangles, each half the size of the next. Draw the symbols listed below above the paper. Place the paper beneath a white (vanilla) candle, a crystal or stone, or a crystal bowl of pure water (with or without a clear crystal within it). You may also place a white candle in a crystal bowl of pure water, and place the triangle in the water or beneath the bowl. Light the candle for twenty-one days in a row.

Allow yourself to be in a meditative state. Acknowledge and dismiss any outside thoughts that may enter into your field of meditation. Just say to yourself, "Oh, there's a thought, I let it go on by." And it vanishes. Such energy of the mental process need not limit your spiritual advancement. Eventually the mind concedes to the soul's desire for peace. "Monkey mind" is a common side effect of our culture in particular, where the mind, rather than the spirit, is the controller.

You may choose to begin the Initiation process with an invocation of your own, or similar to the one on the next page. You may choose to use any word for the Higher Power, knowing that any Name or Expression of God has an Energy and Power of its own.

OPTIONAL: Draw the Power Symbol (3 times) to clear the energy path. Draw the Absentia Symbol which should allow you the ability to transcend all time and space. Draw the Symbol for Universal Consciousness, some call it the Mental Symbol, to connect to Universal Mind. You may also chant "Om" or "Aum" during the process.

Move your attention and intention to the fire at the core of the Solar Plexus Center. Expand the fire outward and upward. Direct the flame and your intention into the High Heart Center. Expand the fire outward and upward. Direct the flame and your intention into the Ajna...the Third Eye Center. Expand the fire outward and upward. Direct the flame and your intention into the Tao Center, through the Soul Star. Expand the fire outward and upward. Direct the flame and your intention into reality. See it happening, sense it happening, feel it happening, know that it is there. It is moved into the power of be-ing. It is actualized. It is so.

The Word
KOTAMA, KOTAMA, KOTAMA

"SO HUM, SO HUM, SO HUM. I am one with the Infinite Divine Light. I AM ONE, I AM ONE, I AM ONE. I am guided by and one with Infinite Intelligence, Infinite Abundance, and boundless Love. I ask for Divine Assistance on this path. I am self-less and free of emotion and insistence. If it is in Divine Order and for the Highest Good, I now invoke Kotama, the Word, to the energy and full expression of the Light. That which I invoke, I invoke for myself and all others if it serves that soul's Divine purpose and Higher Light. That which I speak, through the power of Kotama, I manifest. I am Light becoming and Light is actualized in me and in Divine Purpose of this spoken word. I am a mirror of the Divine Essence as it flows through me and becomes me. What I speak and what I see, I Am, as I release the power of Kotama into my reality and into the reality of Divine Purpose. I release all outcome to Divine Purpose. My spirit is one with Divine Purpose and Action. I am open to the the change of consciousness of needed to manifest my Highest Good. It is so, and so be it. Kotama, Kotama, Kotama." Draw the Symbol for the Word: Kotama.

After you complete this portion of the exercise, move to the "Divine Meditation of So Hum." (Page 86)

Reiki Master Dedication Ceremony

It was the ancient custom for all who aspired to become a Reiki Master to relinquish their former existence and embrace a new life, forsaking all other endeavors except that of service to others. This commitment is for you to decide how you, as a Reiki Master will serve this Planet and all Her sustainable life in Plant and Animal form, Others of Humanity, and Yourself. We leave all that we do in Divine Order, for the Highest Good for Love, Life, Peace, Healing, and Service to the Highest Light.

I COMMIT TO SERVE MOTHER EARTH, HER CREATURES, AND HER PLANT LIFE:

I COMMIT TO SERVE OTHERS OF HUMANITY:

I COMMIT TO SERVE MYSELF:

Make a scroll by rolling this paper with your name visible. At the completion of the ceremony, please retrieve your scroll, take it home and place it in a sacred place. Honor your commitment as best you can.

Please sign your name
_____Date_____

MYSTICISM IN THE MASTERSHIP

In Tibet, there are three classes or types of Masters. The most mystical of these Masters, the "Gongs gyud" teach by telepathy. The other two types of Masters teach by gestures (Da gyud) or speech (Nien ghud). It is felt that there are no longer Masters capable of instructing in the telepathic method, nor students psychically developed enough to grasp the teachings. In the preliminary admission rite to the "Short Path," the novice hears the following:

> "Pass thy way, traveler; stay not here. Many are the pleasant dwellings both in this world and in the others. Live a virtuous life and follow the precepts of the law. Easy and full of charm are the ways that lead to the abodes of bliss. Behind this door is a steep and rugged path, enveloped in gloom. Obstacles, painful to surmount, elusive mirages, exhausting struggles are to be encountered at every step. Is thy foothold sufficiently sure to scale those heights?...Art thou bold enough to face any danger, however perilous?...Art thou wise enough to have destroyed all illusions? Hast thou overcome attachment to life and dost thou feel capable of kindling within thyself the torch which must shed light upon thy path?..."[14]

On that spiritual journey, one may consciously choose to cultivate the mysteries beyond physical recognition, or mysticism. Masters must be certain that the aspiration to mysticism is tempered with the pure understanding that one should not aspire to manipulate others or the Universe. To do so might create Karmic repercussions. Mysticism clearly is not for everyone, and especially not for the ego-centered personality. Mysticism must be balanced with the purity of love's essence.

> "Before practicing the Tantric Yogas that reveal the mind's inherent radiance, mind and body are matured through initiation. Four Sequential empowerments, each associated with progressive levels of subtlety and bliss, activate the practitioner's inner mandala of energy channels and psychic nerves. Purifying the mind stream of subtle obscurations, ini-

---

14. Initiations and Initiates In Tibet, Alexandria David-Neel, Dover Publications, New York, 1993, p. 53

tiation is not always through formal rites, but often arises through potent existential encounters."[15]

"Initiation. Sanskrit abhishekha (Tib. dbang bskur ba) means literally "an anointment, the ritual acknowledgement of a being's assumption of a special transformation, blessing, authority, and responsibility. In Unexcelled Yoga Tantra there are four main initiations, the vase, secret, mind, and the integration of all three to learn, practice, and realize all levels of the Tantric path."[16]

It seems that in the ancient Tibetan traditions, as well as Yoga Tantra, there were four initiations that were imparted in the spiritual journey of the seeker. The notion of initiation involves a "sprinkling" with holy water that links it with baptism and the Hindu rite of the monarchy. The Tibetans on the short path believe that a sacred power enters the body and remains following an initiation.

The four initiations involve different levels, just as in Reiki: 1.) The "Vase" or Vas Empowerment cleanses (much like our clearing cycle) the body of karmic blockages of the psychic channels, and allows one to visualize deities. 2.) The "Mystical" Empowerment cleanses the speech channels and allows the flow of Ki so mantras can be use more powerfully. 3.) The "Divine Knowledge" Empowerment purifies the mind and enhances special practices that transcend the Third Dimension. 4.) The "Absolute" Empowerment is mystical and leads to the discovery of True Mind and Understanding. Following it, symbols can be transcended and subject-object are directly experienced. There is more transmitted in each level of initiation that has never been revealed, and is considered the utmost sacred, between the Lama or Guru and the Tantric adept. If a Reiki Master reads each initiation description closely, they will discover the same Empowerment or energy that is contained in each of the four, sacred, traditional Usui Symbols. Level

15. The Tibetan Art of Healing, Ian Baker, Chronicle Books, San Fransisco, CA, 1997, p. 166
16. The Tibetan Book of The Dead, translated by Robet A.F. Thurman, Bantam Books, New York, 1994, p. 262

Two Practitioners will relate to the first three Empowerments as Symbols.

In Transformational Reiki, if one is already a Reiki Master, I offer a fourth attunement or initiation, which is not of my own device, but rather an ancient ritual involving ancient symbols. This attunement is offered only following personal contemplation and meditation, as I do not feel that it is one that can be taken lightly. We discuss the implications of this initiation in Transformational Reiki Class. The attunement is completely optional. I feel as a Reiki Master my first obligation is first and foremost to the material and application of techniques and teachings. Without wisdom, the energy has no foundation.

I also suggest that Masters always ask for the Next Level of Spiritual Attunement when they are ready for it. This is the"potent existential encounter" that can be activated by the consciousness of the individual. I share that such "encounters" may take many forms, so it is essential that you ask always in Divine Order for the Highest Good, so that if such a step is not appropriate for you in your present state of awareness, it will not transpire. However, when you are ready, you will most certainly be aware of the shift in your consciousness and perhaps even the critical event that precipitated that shift. It is a great gift to a student on the path to the Mastership to be allowed the gift of a physical body to provide the potential leaps desired on the spiritual path. Dr. Tsampa Ngawang shared his thought that enlightenment is only available to one who is in physical form and body: "The body is a mandala. If we look inside, it is an endless source of revelation. Without embodiment there is no foundation from which to gain enlightenment."[17] The Tibetans view hardship and even dis-ease as great opportunities for healing the spirit and releasing karma. In death, the body teaches the greatest of all understandings of the way of the world, that is that all things are impermanent. It is when we try to believe that things are permanent that we suffer. All things are related, and when we forget this essential teaching,

_____

17. Ibid. p. 36

the body suffers an illness. That is what I believe is to blame for the majority of all dis-ease in our current Western culture. We have forgotten that we are a part of all life that we are trampling and destroying in the name of progress. Deepak Chopra shared this philosophy from the Tibetan healing model:

"At the heart of the Tibetan medical tradition is the recognition that the physical world, including our bodies, is largely a product of our individual perception, and that it is the mind that directs the body toward sickness or health...The physician's role within this system is to guide the patient towards greater self-awareness, beyond the self-imposed limitations that foster disease. Ultimately, true healing begins when we discover within ourselves that place where we are linked with the larger forces of the universe. Although each person may seem separate and independent, all of us are connected to patterns of intelligence that govern the whole cosmos. Our bodies are part of a universal body. Our minds an aspect of a Universal Mind." [18]

A Master in the mystical traditions learns to increase subtle power through the invocation of the spoken word, which I call "Kotama." Kotama is also a powerful symbol with the energy of creating or healing. With this is comes a great responsibility. Reiki, to be Reiki, depends upon the Mastership for the continuation of the lineage. It is much like the tradition in Tibet explained by Sogyal Rinpoche: "In our tradition we say that 'three authentics' must be present for the nature of mind to be introduced: the blessing of an authentic master, the devotion of an authentic student, and the authentic lineage of the method of introduction." (The Tibetan Book of Living and Dying, p.43) In Reiki, the transfer of energy, the "authentics" depends upon a physical attunement (blessings) with a physical Reiki Master, a lineage or family tree that represents the direct passage of that energy and the sacred teachings from Master to Master, and the receptivity or openness of the student to accept the attunement and honor the teachings and their Master. The Master is responsible to the lineage, the energy, the sacred teachings, and the student.

---

18. Ibid. p. 8

KOTAMA SCRIPT ONE: THE SOURCE
(OF PHYSICAL PAIN OR DIS-EASE)

SAY TO YOUR CLIENT:

1.) Go down inside your body where we need to go to heal. 5-4-3-2-1. You are there now.

2.) Look around. What do you see, sense, or feel? (Allow them to describe.)

3.) What color is this? (If they have not mentioned color.)

4.) What size is this? (If they have not mentioned size.)

5.) What shape is this? (If they have not mentioned shape.)

6.) How old were you when this first came to you?

7.) See yourself at the age and time that this came to you. See, sense and feel what is happening when this first came to you.

8.) Bring Healing Light into that event. Feel the Healing Light. What color is it?

9.) Bring that same Healing Light into your body where it needs to go. Feel it there and then expand it into a Light of forgiveness. Forgive and then release yourself and all others. Expand the Light and fill all spaces.

10.) If there was any part of you that was lost back then, you will find it now. It will look like something that belonged to you then. Find it and bring it into your heart.

11.) What else do you need to do to heal this?

12.) You are worthy of this Healing Light, and everyday you will say to yourself:

(An affirmation beginning with "I AM...") "I am healed, I am whole, I am well."

Suggested Hand Position: Trans-Point 2   "BHAKTI" (Page 115)

KOTAMA SCRIPT TWO: MENTAL HEALING

1.) You have a special place, like a room in your mind where you store old thoughts and mental patterns.

2.) Let's go to that place in your mind now. 5-4-3-2-1. You are there now.

3.) You see, sense, or feel a black cassette tape there. These are messages from your past.

4.) Listen to that tape for a minute. You hear or sense a message from your past that needs healing now. (You may repeat process as often as needed.)

5.) What is the message?

6.) Who is the message from?

7.) See the younger you that accepted that message as truth.

8.) How old is that younger you?

9.) Talk to that younger you. Hold them close to you, and let them know now what is really true.

10.) Why do you suppose that younger you held onto that message?

11.) Are you and the younger you ready to let go of this message?

12.) Then burn this old tape together, until it is completely gone.

13.) Is there anyone you need to forgive for bringing this message to you?

14.) From the ash of the old black tape, there is a new white tape. It is a message that affirms your new thoughts. It says_____. (Whatever affirmation is needed to balance the negative message...for example, I am smart and other people appreciate and accept my ideas.)

15.) What else do you need to do to feel better and create a positive future?

Note: Children are especially vulnerable to negative suggestions and criticisms because their brains are first in Theta and then later Alpha until their early teens. Suggestions given at these brain wave frequencies make a great impact on the thoughts and mental processes for the rest of one's life.

Suggested Hand Position: Trans-Point 6 "CHITTA" (Page 119)

KOTAMA SCRIPT THREE: EMOTIONAL HEALING

1.) You have emotions that you have stored in your heart and other places in your body.

2.) Let's go down into your heart where we can heal on a deeper level. 5-4-3-2-1. You are there.

3,) The door to your heart is open and the light is on. Step inside your heart.

4.) What color do you see, sense, or feel?

5.) If there is something that needs to be healed, you will see or sense or feel someone or something there, waiting for you.

6.) What is there?

7.) How does that (one) make you feel?

8.) Is there anything that you need to say or do with this (one)? (Forgive?)

9.) Can you let this go now? If you can really let this go, open a door of light in your heart and let this (one) go now. Give them a hug, or whatever you need to do, and let them go. (You may repeat this process as many times as needed.)

10.) Now, look at the walls of your heart. Are there any places that need repaired? Any bruises or holes?

11.) Bring pink (white or gold) Healing Light into the walls of your heart. This is your own Higher Self Energy, like a salve. Fill the spaces with this energy until the walls are solid and the room looks clear.

12.) Feel how light you feel inside. You will remember this feeling and create new Joy in your life from that Light. Say to yourself, "I create joy in my life now."

13.) Is there anything else that needs healed in your heart?

14.) Are there emotions stored anywhere else in your body? (If so, repeat the process.)

Suggested Hand Position: Trans-Point 4 "DAHARA" (Page 117)

KOTAMA SCRIPT FOUR: SPIRITUAL HEALING

1.) You have all kinds of assistance for your healing. You have those who care about you; you have your own ability to heal and reclaim your health, and you have Healing Guides and Angels from the Highest Light (and for the Highest Good).

2.) Are you willing to work with your Healing Assistants?

3.) Sense and feel that a Guide or Angel is with you now. Feel their love and concern for your health and well-being.

4.) Go with them to a special place for healing.

5.) Where are you?

6.) You may now ask them to help you.

7.) Allow them to assist you in recognizing, releasing. and healing the source of all that is needed for you to heal. Just allow it to come to you however it will.

8.) Feel as they apply their Healing Energy to your body, mind, emotions, and spirit.

9.) See, sense, or feel the color, sounds, vibrations, or thoughts that they share with you. Feel and remember the Healing Color or Thoughts.

10.) Allow them to share with you any other information that you need to heal completely.

11.) Do you accept this healing?

12.) Hear your own voice say: "I am healed, I am whole, I am well, and I accept this healing." (Or any other affirmation that you choose to use.)

13.) Thank all who assisted in this healing process.

14.) Know that you can ask at any time for further healing assistance.

Suggested Hand Position: Trans-Point 3 "BRAHMA" or "SURYA" (Page 116)

KOTAMA SCRIPT FIVE: COSMIC BODY HEALING

Note: Items written in parenthesis ( ) are optional according to the client's belief system.

1.) (Your exist and you have always existed.) (You are a product of many lifetimes, past, present, and future.) See , sense, or feel that you are moving down a long hallway with many doors. These doors represent the times before you were born to this life, to this body.

2.) You notice a door ahead of you that is open. It is a door that contains information about habits or patterns that have followed you throughout time.

3.) This information is in the form of a book, photo, or an object that is on the table in the room as you enter it.

4.) Pick up the object on the table. What is it?

5.) Allow yourself to know all that you need to know about this.

6.) Allow a Guide, Master, or Angel to assist you. (Another door opens. This door leads to a most recent lifetime when this habit or pattern was present. Step through the door and look down at your feet. What are you wearing on your feet? Look around you. What do you see? Go to the most important time in that lifetime.) Experience all that you need to know to heal this pattern or habit (or Karma).

7.) Do you need to forgive anyone? Does anyone need to forgive you?

8.) Send healing energy to your past.

9.) Affirm: "Through all time, past, present, and future, and through all dimensions, I now accept assistance and guidance in healing old patterns, thoughts, (Karma) and habits. I bring Healing Light into all levels and all forms of my existence."

10.) (Light a white candle in that room for further healing and Light.) Come out of the room and shut the door.

11.) Come back up the hallway to this room, to this time.

Suggested Hand Position: Trans Point 1 "AVIDYA" (Page 112)

KOTAMA SCRIPT SIX: LIGHT BODY HEALING

Note: Items in parenthesis ( ) are optional according to the client's belief system.

1.) (The ego is what keeps us separate from other forms of life.) You are much more than a physical being having a spiritual experience. (from Deepak Chopra)

2.) You are walking on a path to a meadow. In the center of that meadow is an ancient oak tree.

3.) You sit on the ground in front of the tree. Call to you each aspect of your ego-personality hiding behind the tree that you are ready to recognize and heal. These aspects of you may not look like you at all, but mirror the energy of that part of your ego awareness.

4.) Each aspect has a name. Ask each one, "What is your name?" (The names may represent emotions as Fear, Anger, Doubt, Rejection, and so on.) The names represent the energy within the ego that needs attention or healing.

5.) Each aspect has an age. Ask each what age they are. (This represents the energy's birth into your ego.)

6.) As each aspect reveals itself to you, embrace it if you can, and bring Light, Love, and Acceptance into the heart of each part of you. (Some ego aspects may represent your "Shadow Self" and may be difficult to recognize...may even appear unattractive, and difficult to embrace.) Embrace, integrate, and heal these aspects of your ego. Bring them into the center of your High Heart.

7.) Affirm: "I bring Healing Light and Love into all aspects of my ego to integrate and lift these aspects to a vibration of Higher Light and Love."

8.) Stand and embrace the tree. Notice how there is no difference between you and the tree. The tree's strength is your strength. You are one with the sun, the wind, and all of nature. You are whole, healed, and free!

Suggested Hand Position: Trans-Point 2 "BHAKTI" Or Trans-Point 3 "BRAHMA" or "SURYA" (Page 116)

KOTAMA SCRIPT SEVEN:
INTERDIMENSIONAL BODY EXPANSION

1.) See sense, and feel that you are unlimited. You are limitless in form, expression, time, dimension, and space. You the Divine form of Light Essence.

2.) As you expand your awareness first inward, and then outward, allow each of your chakras to become clear, to harmonize, and then radiate and expand outward into the cosmos. (May say radiate, radiate, radiate...)

3.) Breathe Light into the red of the Root Center. Clear, Harmonize, Radiate.

Breathe Light into the orange of the Sacral Center. Clear, Harmonize, Radiate.

Breathe Light into the yellow of the Solar Plexus. Clear, Harmonize, Radiate.

Breathe Light into the emerald of the Heart. Clear, Harmonize, Radiate.

Breathe Light into the turquoise of the High Heart. Clear, Harmonize, Radiate.

Breathe Light into the blue of the Throat. Clear, Harmonize, Radiate.

Breathe Light into the indigo of the Third Eye. Clear, Harmonize, Radiate.

Breathe Light into the violet of the Crown. Clear, Harmonize, Radiate.

Breathe Light into the silver of the Soul Star. Clear, Harmonize, Radiate.

Breathe Light into the gold of the Tao Center. Clear, Harmonize, Radiate.

Breathe Light into the white of the Interdimensional Center. Merge with Energy.

4.) Feel and sense all colors merging and creating the ultimate harmony of one color, one Light.

5.) Feel that Light moving out into the expansiveness of the Cosmos.

6.) Feel that Light radiating far beyond the Self.

7.) Float in timelessness and absorb the Higher Vibration of Infinite Light. Feel the Peace, Sense the Peace, and be the Peace. You are one with the Universe.

8.) Stay in that space as long as as is appropriate. Then return easily and effortlessly to the present moment, to the eternal now. **Suggested Hand Position: Any point.**

TIME TRAVEL AND REIKI HEALING

In Transformational Reiki, there is a process that we teach that involves the power of the symbol that transcends all space and time. It is a method used in Absentia Healing or with the client present and aware. However, we do not allow them to see the drawing of the sacred symbols that we use. The client can travel back in time to restore the body's original blueprint for wellness and wholeness. It involves another use of Kotama, or the power of the spoken word. During the treatment, we arrive at the site of a specific healing opportunity. We place our hands on the healing opportunity site and/or the High Heart Center. We utilize three of the four Usui symbols, invoking Universal Consciousness, and transcending space and time. We then ask the client to journey back to a time when the body was well and whole. They may even go back into a past life, as in the case of karmic dis-ease, or into the womb with prenatal emotions absorbed or transferred from the mother. Ask them:

1.) Where are you? 2.) How old are you? 3.) What happened to create this dis-ease? 4.) What do you need to do to heal this? Then ask them to restore the original blueprint of wellness that existed prior to the dis-ease.

I have even used the time travel technique on the Interdimensional Level, where a client's journey led them to another place, time, and space beyond Earth for their healing potential. An Interdimensional healing opportunity generally defies all rational explanations for its existence.

When the client retrieves the original blueprint for healing, the intention is to recover and then restore the soul's original purpose. In Tibet, major life-threatening diseases are believed to be warnings that you are not attentive to your spiritual life.

UTILIZING THE KOTAMA SCRIPTS
FOR TRANS-REIKI

1.) Begin at the Crown with the sacred mudra of Healing. (Lace fingers on outside of knuckles, then point index fingers and thumbs forward toward the crown center of the client.)

2.) When connected, begin with the sacred symbols of _____ and _____ at the crown center. Press in and hold one of two positions for several minutes:

      A.) Left hand at back of occiput, right hand on center top of head.

      B.) Left hand on crown, right hand on forehead.

3.) Introduce the Mantra Breathing to your client. (Note: you do not have to call this Mantra Breathing to your more conservative clients.) Ask them to breathe in _____ (mantra) and breathe out _____ (mantra). I usually ask people to "Breathe in peace and breathe out Light." You may participate in this Mantra Breathing technique as well.

4.) Focus on your breathing, and move into the Level of the Unisonium. (See previous pages for moving into the Unisonium.)

5.) Move to the appropriate Kotama Script.

6.) The next hand placement should be at the place of healing opportunity. When you instruct your client to go to a place for physical, emotional, mental, or spiritual healing, for example: "go into the body where you need to go to heal," or "go to the place in your mind...," or "move down into your heart," then that is where you place your hands if you can. If the healing opportunity site is in an awkward place, or a place that you would not like someone to place their hands on you, then hold your hands above the area, not touching.

7.) See, sense, or feel a healing color that is flowing through you to them.

8.) Follow other hand placements as you are guided to do so. For example, you may choose to focus upon the Liver for Emotional Healing, or for physical healing, the eyes are related to the health of the kidneys. Sweep and seal.

KOTAMA: RELEASING ADDICTIONS FROM THE SPIRITUAL BODY

In the half-hour pretalk prior to the Reiki session, I generally ask my client who has come for assistance to release addictions, "On a scale of one to ten, how badly do you want to let go of your addiction?" If the answer is less than six, I will suggest that perhaps they are not yet committed to the energy and discipline that is essential to release addictions. In other words, we may release the energy of the addiction in the Spiritual Body, but the rest is up to them. They must continue to work with the Physical Body by allowing into the body only that which best honors the body. They might even consider a week of supervised fasting. They must work with the Mental Body in allowing only positive thoughts. The emotional body must be nurtured in constructive rather than destructive ways. There must be full co-operation on all levels of being. If you are comfortable in doing so, ask your client if they feel that there is a Spiritual Power greater than they are. If so, you might call upon assistance of that energy or energies to assist in the releasing process. If not, allow them to know that they have a "Higher Self" or a "Future Self" who can assist. There must also be present the energy of what might be called "Grace to release karma," as well as the energy of Forgiveness. The client should rest for one to three days following the session.

KOTAMA SCRIPT TO RELEASE ADDICTIONS FROM SPIRITUAL BODY

1.) See, sense, and feel that all who love you are with you now, including _____(the Greater Spiritual Power). Are They here with you? (Pause)

2.) As you take in three deep breaths, breathe in peace and as you breathe out, let go. Breathe out all of that old fear, doubt, anger, lack of self-love and distrust, denial, pain, frustration that you held deep inside. As you breathe this out, sense that it is a darkness. A darkness that has a shape, a size, and maybe even a name or a face.

3.) How big is this shape? Describe it to me.

4.) Where do you suffer or feel this energy in your body? (If it is appropriate, you move to that location and apply Reiki energy.)

5.) Bring all of your addictive behaviors and energy now up into your own two hands Right where it exists. (Where your hands are.) Focus all of your energy into bringing that energy into your hands.

6.) Ask _____(Greater Spiritual Power) to assist you in bringing up all of that addictive energy up and into your hands so we can release it. It will all go when you decide to release it. Is it all there?

7.) Now bring it higher, up away from your body. (Practitioner places their two hands around hands of the client. Practitioner draws appropriate symbols over client's hands.) Are you willing to forgive yourself and any others?

8.) In a minute, I want you to say the words "go, go, go" with great conviction in order to release this energy. Then I will clap the outside of your hands.

9.) Through the Power of Grace and with Divine Intervention, I ask that these energies that are not serving _____'s Highest Good now be released.   Now say "go" aloud three times. (Practitioner takes deep Golden breath. With third "go" Practitioner blows breath on hands and claps. Sweep three times.)

10.) I want you to breathe in 3 breaths of Violet Light, energy of your own soul returning.

11. Optional: Practitioner may chant three times: "Gate, Gate, Paragate, parasamgate, Bodi svaha." (Got a{long a}, Got a, Para got a, parasom gat a, Bodi svaha) This means: "Gone, gone, all is gone, enlightenment!"

12.)   When you are ready, you may open your eyes. How do you feel?

(Practitioner seals in the healing, and gives thanks to all who assisted in the procedure.)

KOTAMA AND TRANS-REIKI
MANTRA BREATHING
©1997 KARYN MITCHELL

A mantra can transmute and transform energy. For example, if a person is angry, the use of a mantra at the time of anger can transform the anger into compassion. It can transform fear into calm awareness. It is useful at the time of death to shift the consciousness to the spiritual plane of existence. For example, when Gandhi was shot and dying, he repeated the word, "Rama," which is the Hindu word for God. The general purpose of a mantra is to raise the vibration beyond negative energy or emotions. Many religions use mantras as a form of mental focus upon the Divine. Our purpose in Mantra Breathing is to move to another level in preparation for healing.

In the book , <u>The Unstruck Bell, Powerful Strategies for Using a Mantram</u>, by Eknath Easwaran, explains how to use a mantra:

"A mantram--or mantra, as it is often called--is a powerful spiritual formula, which, when repeated silently in the mind, has the capacity to transform consciousness. There is nothing magical about this. It is simply a matter of practice. The mantram is a short, powerful spiritual formula for the highest power that we can conceive of--whether we call it God, or the ultimate reality, or the self within. Whatever the name we use, with the mantram we are calling up what is best and deepest within ourselves. The mantram has appeared in every major spiritual tradition, West and East, because it fills a deep, universal need in the human heart."

Select a mantram that appeals to you. Every religious tradition has a mantram, often more than one. But you needn't subscribe to any religion to benefit from the mantram--you simply have to be willing to try it. For Christians, the name of Jesus itself is a powerful mantram, Catholics also use 'Hail Mary', or 'Ave Maria.' Jews may use 'Barukh attah adonai'; Muslims use the name of Allah or Allahu akbar. Probably the oldest Buddhist mantram is 'Om mani padme hum.' And in Hinduism, among many choices, I recommend 'Rama, Rama,' which was Mahatma Gandhi's mantram."

"Once you have chosen your mantram, do not change it. If

you do, you will be like a person digging shallow holes in many places; you will never go deep enough to find water." [19]

The following mantras and their backgrounds also come from information found in <u>The Unstruck Bell</u>, pgs. 37-56:

Christian Tradition: "Jesus" (to ask Jesus for assistance and to be more like Him. "Yesu Christu," or "Om Yesu Christu" (from Hindu Christians), "Lord Jesus Christ, have mercy on us." (or "Lord Jesus Christ"), from the Catholic tradition, "Hail Mary...," from "the Way of the Pilgrim," there is in the Russian tradition the words, "Gospodi pomilui," "Lord have mercy." In the Greek Orthodox tradition there is: "Kyrie emon, Iesou Christe, Yie Theou, eleison ymas" which means "Lord of ours, Jesus Christ, Son of God, have mercy on us."

Mysticism in India brings us the mantras: "Rama" which means, "he who fills us with abiding joy." "'The Rule of Rama' is a phrase that Gandhi took from the Hindu scriptures, and refers to a kingdom in which the love we have for one another is never diminished, a kingdom ruled by justice, not violence. When we repeat the mantram Rama, Rama, Rama, we are asking that this kingdom of heaven be established here on earth."[20] The mantram of Swami Ramdas of India is: "Om Sri Ram jai jai Ram, which means "May joy prevail." One of the best know mantras in India combines three names of the Lord:

"Hare Rama Hare Rama
Rama Rama Hare Hare,
Hare Krishna, Hare Krishna,
Krishna Krishna Hare Hare."[21]

"Hare means, 'he who steals our hearts'. Krishna means 'he who draws us to himself."[22] In southern India, "Om namah Shivaya" is often used as an example of "I honor the Divine within." "Om mani padme hum" is the mantra of power of the Avalokitesvara Bodhisattva (Kuan Yin, the goddess of compassion).

---

19. <u>The Unstruck Bell</u>, Eknath Easwaran, 1977, Nilgiri Press, p. 8-9
20. Ibid. p. 43
21. Ibid. p. 45
22. Ibid. p. 45

In the Hasidic Jewish tradition, the mantram, "Ribo shel-olam," which means Lord of the Universe, is used.

In the Muslim tradition, the words, "Bismillah ir-rahman" means, "in the name of Allah, the merciful, the compassion-ate." Also used are the words, "Allah," or "Allahu akbar" (God is great).

The syllables "Om" or "Aum" refer to a high vibrational en-ergy. "Om" symbolizes the nature of God beyond all names and realities. "Aum" I understand, stands for states of aware-ness, the "A" stands for the waking state, the "U" stands for dreaming, and the "M" stands for deep sleep.

John Blofeld states:

"Thousands of Tibetans use mantras effectively for yogic purposes every day, whereas 'magical' effects upon external objects are now rare--although, unless one discounts a good deal of evidence, they are not unknown even in this day and age. It would seem that most lamas either do not know or else prefer not to teach certain shabdic (sacred sound) secrets per-taining to the miraculous use of mantras. If one is to assume that, in former times, these secrets were more widely taught than now, that would explain why there are so many refer-ences to 'magical' mantric operations in Tibetan literature."[23]

There were sacred mantras invoked for their healing prop-erties, sacred mantras for religious practice and praise, prepa-ration for birth and death, and sacred mantras for the attain-ment of Enlightenment.

Mata Amritanandamayi, "Ammachi," or "Amma" as she is respectfully called, is a Satguru, a God-Realized Soul and Hindu saint. Information from a pamphlet from her organization en-titled, "Mantra, The Significance and Practice of Repeating the Divine Name" states:

"These Sanskrit mantras have a unique power of their own. The most basic, though certainly not the least important func-tion of the mantra, is as a tool to focus and quiet the mind. When one repeats these sacred divine sounds, one invokes spiritual energy which will purify one's thoughts, feelings, and

---

23. Mantras, Sacred Words of power, John Blofeld, 1977, New York, E.P. Dutton and Co., p. 102

one's whole being, blessing one with peace and divine qualities. Ultimately the mantra can serve as a ladder to God, to the realization of our True Nature."

To choose a mantra oneself is perfectly fine. Those who worship Jesus may find that they like to repeat His name. A Hindu child born into a family of Krishna devotees may automatically begin to sing "Hare Krishna," and thousands of Tibetans grow up with "Om Mani Padme Hum" ever on their lips. Whether it comes automatically, prompted by our heritage or upbringing, or whether we actively seek out a suitable mantra, makes no difference. If it is used properly, repeated with concentration and love, it can only serve one well."

"Nearly all of Mother's mantras begin with OM, a mantra in itself, which is said to be the manifest symbol of the cosmic vibration, or God. They also each contain a bijaksara (bija+aksara, seed+indestructible), a sacred syllable associated with a particular deity. Each of these syllables (products of sages' meditation) is the actual embodiment of the energy and qualities of the deity it represents. When a bijaksara (or entire mantra) is chanted with concentration, one gets attuned to the energy of that deity, as the essence of that deity and the cosmic sound are the same. .."

"A mantra should neither be seen or heard by anyone else. For a mantra to be effective, it must be chanted religiously every day. It may also be chanted mentally while one is involved in mundane tasks. Waiting in line, driving, walking, house cleaning, bathing, etc. are also ideal times to repeat the mantra. The more one chants the mantra, the more one is able to realize its purifying effects."

If you do not have a personal mantra, you may choose an ancient one, or create one with your own energy. It is best to seek the assistance of a Guide or Divine Master through the power of meditation. Many believe that you must be initiated with or into a mantra for it to have any power for you. This is especially true in Hinduism, where a Master must train for many years to obtain a level of initiating others to the power of mantra. I have guided students to find their own personal mantra, if there is no hope for them of finding a Master, and many times it involves the energy or focus that is part of their soul's purpose. In such cases, the mantra assumes a role more like a positive affirmation. Yogananda states:

"During all affirmations, your attention should be centered in the spot between the eyebrows; during thought affirmations, in the medulla oblongata, and during devotional affirmations, in the heart. At appropriate times man automatically fixes his mind one of these psychological regions; for example, during states of emotion he feels the heart center to the exclusion of all other parts of the body. By the practice of affirmations one acquires the power of consciously directing his attention to the vital sources of will, thought, and feeling...Absolute, unquestioning faith in God is the greatest method of instantaneous healing."[24]

"DIVINE MEDITATION OF SO HUM"
THE POWER OF THE BREATH OF LIFE

"Hamsah" is the Sanskrit seed word for "So Hum." It means, "I Am Divine" or "I Am That." It is the sound of the breath, the sound of life. If you wish to manifest peace, you could utilize the word, "Shanti," which means "peace." As you breathe in, you breathe in "So," as you exhale, you exhale with "Hum." If you are using "Shanti," you inhale "Shan," and exhale "ti." This is the meditation technique taught to me twenty some years ago by a Buddhist Nun. Transcendental Meditation (T.M.) uses a similar method to harmonize the soul with the breath.

1.) Feel the golden fire of the Central Sun glowing in your Solar Plexus Center expanding outward into your auric field.

24. <u>Scientific Healing Affirmations</u>, Paramahansa Yogananda Self-Realization Fellowship, LosAngeles, p.44-45

2.) Feel your golden aura expand outward filling the room and the space around you.

3.) With each breath, consciousness expands and moves outward to the Universe.

4.) Begin to silently chant the "So" on the inhale, and "Hum" on the exhale.

5.) Move your awareness upward through crown and ascend the 11 Golden Steps.

6.) Create your Manifestation Center, and see a Golden Chest or box.

7.) Place your Divine Intention into the Golden Chest.

8.) Drink from the Golden Chalice of Pure Love and Light.

9.) Affirm: "Light is in me. I am worthy of that," "I AM THAT, SO HUM".

10.) Continue So Hum breathing as long as peace resides within you.

11.) Come down the 11 Steps and into your body.

12.) Give thanks to all who assisted in this process, including your Higher Self.

PRANAYAMA COLOR BREATHING

Meditation for balance: Place index finger and second finger of your dominant hand upon your Ajna Center (Third Eye between eyebrows). Rest your thumb on one side of your nose and your ring finger on the other side. Press your right nostril close. Breathe in the color violet through your open left nostril. Breathe this color all the way down to your navel. (Solar Plexus/ Sacral Centers). As you exhale, exhale the color white. Breathe in two more deep breaths of violet. (Exhale white) Release the right nostril and press the left nostril close. Breathe in three deep breaths, breathing in the color blue and exhaling the color white. Release the left nostril and breathe in deeply three times through both nostrils, breathing in the color white and exhaling the color white. Sense that you have been purified and completely balanced by your breath. Prana is not only the basic life force, but is also the original creative power.

THE INVOCATION OF OTHER CHANTS
OR MANTRAS

If you wish to expand beyond the twelve steps and into the consciousness of one of the world's oldest religions, you might add one or more of the following mantras from Jainism. The religious tradition of Jainism began more than 2,500 years ago in India.

"The term is derived form the Sanskrit 'Jina' --"'conqueror', which means conquest over bondage imposed by the phenomenal world. Souls are beginningless and endless, eternally individual. It classes souls into three broad categories: those that are not yet evolved, those in the process of evolution, and those that are liberated, free from rebirth...Jainism is, above all, a religion of love and compassion."[25]

Three Ancient Jain Mantras may be added to complete this process :

---

25. Internet: http//www.interinc.com/Allfaiths/Jainism/

FORGIVENESS MANTRA

Khaamemi Savve Jivaa
Savve Jivaa Khamantu Mai
Mitti Mai Savva bhuesu
Veram majjham na Kenai

Translation of the Forgiveness Mantra:
    "I forgive all the living beings of the universe, and may all the living-beings forgive me for my faults. I do not have any animosity towards anybody, and I have friendship for all the living beings."

JAM JAM MANEN

Jam Jam Manen Badham
Jam Jam Vaayen Bhaasiyam Pavam
Jam Jam Kaayen Kadam
Tassa Michaami Dukkadam

Translation of the Jam Jam Mahen:
    "If I have done wrong, or collected bad Karmas by my mind, speech, and body, I wish to be forgiven and my sins nullified."

MANTRA

Aum Hrim Shrim Klim Arhum Hamsah

Translation of Mantra:
    "Aum is the Divine name of God.
Hrim is the seed mantra representing all Divine Goddesses.
Shrim is the seed for the Goddess of prosperity.
Klim removes all poisons and sins.
Arhum is the name of God.
Hamasah means (So Hum) I Am Divine."

---

26. Internet: Pratikram Rituals for Young Adults of North America.
http://sunsite.unc.edu/jainism/philosophy/rituals/prtknml.txt

In India one of the favorite mantrams is the recitation of the 3 names of the Lord:

HARE RAMA HARE RAMA
RAMA RAMA HARE HARE
HARE KRISHNA HARE KRISHNA
KRISHNA KRISHNA HARE HARE

GAYATRI MANTRA

Aum Bhoor Bhuwah Swaha
Tat Savitur Varenyam
Bhargo Devasya Dheemahi
Dhiyo Yo Naha Prachodayat

Translation of the Gayatri Mantra:
"Oh God! Thou art the Giver of Life, Remover of pain and sorrow. The Bestower of happiness. Oh Creator of the Universe, May we receive thy supreme sin-destroying Light. May Thou guide our intellect in the right direction."[27]

THE HEART SUTRA is described as the unequaled mantra, the allayer of all suffering, whose austere meaning is: "Gone, gone, gone beyond, gone wholly beyond--Enlightenment!" It is the invocation of transcendental wisdom. It is one of my favorites.

The Heart Sutra ends with the most powerful mantra:
Gate Gate Paragate, parasamgate bodi svaha.

OM NAMAHA SHIVAYA[29]
Translation of Om Namaha Shivaya:

" I honor the Divine Within." It invokes the personification of

---

27. Internet: Aimani Homepage, Extracted from "The Great Science and Philosphy of Gayatri", by Shree Ram Sharma Achrya, Shanti Kunj, Hardwaar, Uttar Pradesh, India.
28. Ibid.

the Hindu Trinity in the principles of creation, preservation, and destruction. We call upon Shiva, the destroyer to eliminate our selfish nature and our sense of separateness. We are reminded that pain and growth often come hand in hand. Suffering becomes a sign of grace.

"Now that particular mantra, "Om," is one that melts you into the sound. You don't stay separate from the "Om," you keep disappearing into it. Other mantras are part of devotional practices that are dualistic in their nature--that is, they concern your relationship with the divine. Those mantras don't celebrate your love for the divine from the space of your separateness. Devotion works through the medium of your love, and the dance becomes the dialogue between Lover and Beloved the separate entity relating to the One through love..." "So there are ways that song can open us to other dimensions of being. Spiritual, devotional uses of sound that are familiar in many other cultures, but that we're just beginning to explore here in the west. As you work with these practices, you'll find that an even deeper part of the process starts to emerge. You'll arrive at a place in which you're listening not only to the sound, but to the matrix of silence from within which the sound arises. You're resting in the silence, and the sound is creating itself. The sounds are rising, and you're just sitting there, in the still center of the silence. That's when sound will have transcended itself, through the practice of song." (by Ram Dass)[29]

Note: You may purchase these two chants on C.D. or cassette tape. "The Gayatri Mantra" is narrated by Ghanshyam Singh Birla, music by Peter Keogh and Serge Fiori. Galaxy Recordings, 351 Victoria Avenue, Westmount, Quebec H3Z 2N1, Canada. "Om Namaha Shivaya" by Robert Gass and On Wings of Song, Spring Hill Music, Bx 800 Boulder Colorado.

29.Ibid

"NAMU MYOHO RENGE KYO"

Translation of Namu Myoho Renge Kyo: "Sacred title and essence of the Lotus Sutra."[30] By chanting, we receive all of Buddha's practices, love, and compassion.

The Lotus Sutra can be invoked in its entirety by merely chanting its title. In fact, it is considered "daimoku," or "great title." Chanting "Namu Myoho Renge Kyo" is called a "daimoku." The Lotus Sutra contains 69,384 characters in its eight volumes. It defines our own personal life in terms of Buddha's life, and we become a reflection of that behavior and wisdom. One passage from the Lotus Sutra reads: "In the latter days of the law, when the law is about to perish, a person who embraces this Sutra will be carrying out all forms of service to the Buddha. It asks the question, can one become Buddha by chanting "Namu Myoho Renge Kyo?" It is a question of faith.

OTHER DIVINE TRADITIONS

If you have learned other chants in your own traditions, you may consider invoking them into the processes of your meditation. There is a beautiful recording of "The Joyful and Glorious Mysteries of the Most Holy Rosary" and "The Sorrowful Mysteries of the Most holy Rosary and the Chaplet of Divine Mercy," sung throughout with musical accompaniment by Jim Cowan.

Most everyone can remember the seemingly mysterious impact of the power of "CHANT," the recording of various Catholic chants by the Benedictine Monks of Santo Domingo. The world was ready in 1994 to have its vibration raised in songs of devotion. It was best seller on the music charts for some time.

Recordings of all faiths can be found on the market. "The Maha Mrityunjaya Mantra" is also available on the Galaxy Recording La-

30. "Namu Myoho Renge Kyo", Nichiren Buddhist Fellowship, (510-652-7090)

bel, 1994. "Tibetan Chants-Buddhist Meditation" by Lama Karta is available through BMG Music and Milan Entertainment, 1996. Another is "Tibetan Sacred Temple Music" by Shing Star Productions.

One of my personal chant favorites is called "The Eternal Om", by Robert Slap, Valley of the Sun, Box 38, Malibu, CA 90265. From that C.D. jacket cover: "The OM is all sound and silence throughout time, the roar of eternity and the essence of pure beings. It invokes the ALL that is otherwise inexpressible and it is the highest spiritual sound on earth."

OM MANI PADME HUM is the ancient Buddhist Mantram that invokes the "jewel in the lotus of the heart." The heart is the lotus, and the jewel is the joy and peace waiting there to be uncovered. The lotus flower is symbolic as it grows from the mud into a beautiful, fragrant flower, much as our hearts can bloom compassion from our own muddy past. As we recite this mantra, we are encouraging the lotus to bloom. It is the Bodhisattva of Compassion (Chenrezi) himself in the form of sound. There is no difference between the deity and the sound of the mantra. It purifies negativity and karmic obscurations that prevent us from meeting Chenrezi. It is called the "Mani." You may find it most useful to recite your own personal, selected mantras for at least twenty one days consecutively.

NAMU DAI BOSA All dimensions are condensed into the words of this sutra:

"This untouchable, unthinkable, universal world is each one of us; not only each one of us, but each of our cells. Do you know how many cells there are in your body? ...a scholar has said there are seventeen billion cells in the human body. And, of course, in addition to these cells there are electrons and other smaller elements-small, small, endlessly small....Each such thing-no matter how small--is a sentient being. This is the meaning of 'dai.' As a character, 'dai' (great) is usually considered the opposite of smallness. But since the true meaning of 'dai' is absolute,' in even the smallest thing there is 'dai.' Bosa means 'enlightened one.' You are all such wonderful persons. This is Buddha!...There is no need to think about endless-dimension universal worlds. Just 'namu dai bosa.' Just 'mu.' Just breathing. Just counting. Nothing else. Just...!" (From a talk by Nakagawa Soen Roshi, Zen Studies Society.)

By reciting this mantra, we become the embodiment of a bodhisattva. It is said to be the representation of all of the Sutras, as it condenses everything. It is called "mu."

NAMU AMIDA BUTSU "Praise (Namu) to the Buddha of Infinite Life." Butsu means Buddha in Japanese. "Nembutsu" is to abandon the self by repeating the mantra "namu amida butsu." The Amida Buddha lives within all of life, but remains a stranger to us until we become conscious of its presence. When we realize that this Buddha is there, it replaces the lower ego in life and rises to the higher place where it is can rule.

The Sanskrit word "Mantra" is a tool to focus the mind and quiet it. "Man" means "To think," and "tra" means "tool." It is the use and creation of a particular energy through recitation and repetition. There can be many purposes of and for this energy. It has intention. For example, one intention might be to purify karma, thoughts, negative feelings, or the being as a whole. It can act as a blessing, or can help one to realize their maximum potential in this lifetime. As a spiritual formula, a mantra can transform consciousness. The Dalai Lama observes total silence until he has recited his mantra to consecrate speech, so that his words throughout the day will all be positive. It can invoke Divine Assistance on our behalf both from within us and beyond us. Some select a mantra, others are gifted a mantra by a Guru or Great Being. Sometimes a mala is used to assist in the process of repeating a mantra 108 times or more. In his book, <u>The Unstruck Bell</u>, Eknath Easwaran explains to us the power of consistent practice with a mantra:

"From the very first day you begin to use the mantram, it begins to grow in your consciousness. It germinates like the tiny seed that will eventually grow into a magnificent tree, and as you repeat it often and enthusiastically, it sends its roots deeper and deeper. Over a period of years, it you have been practicing all the other spiritual disciplines which strengthen your will and deepen your concentration, the taproot of the mantram will extend fathoms deep, where it works to unify your consciousness--resolving old conflicts, solving problems you may not even be aware of, and transforming negative emotions into spiritual energy.

Finally, when this mantram root reaches the bedrock of consciousness, you become established in the mantram. It has become an integral part of your being, permeating your consciousness from the surface level down to the very depths. Then it is no longer necessary to repeat the mantram; it goes on repeating itself, echoing continuously at the very deepest levels of the mind. This is what Saint Paul means when he exhorts to us to 'pray without ceasing.' As a Sufi mystic says,

'Those who heard this word by the ear alone let it go out by the other ear; but those who heard it with their souls imprinted it on their souls and repeated it until it penetrated their hearts and souls, and their whole being became this word.'" (p. 209-210)

MANTRA AND MALA MEDITATION

A mala is a tool used by some in mantra meditation. The word, "mala" means a garland or string of flowers, and refers to a string of beads that eventually add up to 108. My favorite mala is made of 54 rudraksha seeds (rudraksha means "tears of the Buddha"), so I turn the mala after completion of the first circle and complete another cycle. According to Guru Kirn Kaur Khalsa, there are many advantages to meditating with a mala:

"You can reduce stress and anxiety (e.g., enhance wisdom, prosperity, patience, health, and communication) and direct the body and mind to Infinity to burn karma for a happy future. This is achieved through the power of mantra, healing aspects of semi-precious stones and the stimulation of specific meridian points in the fingers as the beads are moved across them...By creating a vibration, a sound current, you affect other vibrations (atoms).

By projecting the mind to Infinity and stimulating certain meridians in the nervous system, you can change your karma and your destiny. Ancient Yogic knowledge has known for centuries that the body has the power to heal itself, that we can play an active role in shaping our destinies; physically, mentally, and spiritually." ("Mala Meditation" p. 1)

As you repeat the mantra, you use the mala as a means to count each repetition. This is called "Japa," or repeat. When a mantra is spoken softly or whispered, as most people do in private, it is called mantra. When spoken very loudly, it is called "kirtan." Moving the tongue in the mouth stimulates the meridians. The mantra or mala meditation in any form neutralizes negative thoughts and forces. Begin with the head bead, calming and chanting OM three times. It is best to project the mantra from the naval level and pull the beads over the heart finger, the second finger with the thumb. Focus and listen to your words.

COLOR AND LIGHT THERAPY APPLICATIONS
What I call "REIKI IRO"

Color acupuncture and acupressure is gaining widespread use, especially in Europe.

In Reiki, we can channel specific color applications to assist in the healing process, or we can directly apply the color(s) needed to the chakra area. Color is merely a property of Light. The American Heritage Dictionary defines color as: "That aspect of things that is caused by differing qualities of the light reflected or emitted by them. It might be be defined in terms of the observer, or of the light." Color then might be called the perception of the vibrational rate. The application of color as a vibrational field can then accelerate healing. It is an adjunct to the healing process. In his book, Light: Medicine of the Future, Jacob Liberman suggests that certain (or all) dis-eases may be caused by a lack of a particular color essence in a person's life, or the lack of the body's ability to absorb these certain colors. I know of a man who worked with Liberman in an attempt to restore his deteriorating vision. Liberman performed a series of chromatic tests and determined that this individual needed the color of teal blue to heal his eyes. The irony is that this individual had surrounded himself in this color for the past three years: his room was painted teal, his clothes were teal, and even his car was teal! He couldn't get enough teal, and instinctively he was directed to this color. So he started to wear teal-colored glasses specially designed to wear for a certain number of hours a day. In the past, I have personally used colored "Chakra Glasses" to balance my own chakras, or to add color (yellow) on winter days when the skies were not sunny. This really assisted with my Seasonal Affective Disorder. However, I did find that if I did not need a particular color, I became anxious when I attempted to apply that color of glasses, particularly when driving a car. It was much like the north poles of two magnets repelling each other. If I needed a particular color, I was attracted to it and was comfortable wearing those glasses. This is much like opposite poles of a magnet, north-south polarities attracting each other. It is also reflective of the Yin-Yang balance. If an energy system or a chakra "needs" a particular color, then it is what we could call deficient, or empty, "Kyo." It it is excessive or "overcrowded" in a particular color, that causes an imbalance in the Yin/Yang balance called "Jitsu." You must then tonify or balance Kyo by filling it with the same color, and disperse Jitsu with opposing color applications. You tonify color application of Kyo by applying the same color. You disperse Jitsu by applying the opposite of that chakra's color. On the following page are listed the colors of the Interdimensional Chakras (from Root to Interdimensional) to tonify, and their opposite colors for dispersing.

There are many ways to bring color into the chakras. You may apply stones if you have their permission, and if the energies of the stones are the optimum color balance mechanism for that individual. Otherwise, you can directly channel color essence with your thoughts by concentrating upon the vibration of that color. (Energy follows intention.) Another means to balance the chakras with color is to cut triangles of fabric in the color spectrums needed. I suggest three inch equilateral triangles. Apply these triangles, points up toward the head, to the chakra area where color therapy is needed. Any centers above the crown go above the crown in their appropriate order. You might use stones. You might also suggest that the individual wear that color or utilize it in visualizations (such as breathing in color) or affirmations. Drinking lunar or solar infusions of water in colored containers also brings color essence into the vital life force and nurtures all bodies.

REIKI IRO: CHAKRA COLOR APPLICATIONS

CHAKRA	KYO	JITSU
Root:	Red	Green
Sacral:	Orange	Blue
Solar Plexus:	Yellow	Violet
Leydes:	Saffron	Blue-Violet
Heart:	Green	Red
High Heart:	Turquoise	Red-Orange
Throat:	Blue	Orange
Ajna (Third Eye):	Indigo	Yellow-Orange
Crown:	Violet	Yellow
Soul Star:	Silver	Metallic Black
Tao:	Gold	Ultraviolet
Interdimensional:	White	Black

ENERGIES OF KYO AND JITSU IMBALANCES

Chakra	Kyo (Deficient)	Jitsu (Excess)
Root:	Manipulative	Aggressive
Sacral:	Flighty, Shy, low libido	Openly sexual, Selfish
Solar Plexus:	Stay in the shadows	Unable to manifest; control issues
Leydes:	Lack of self-reliance	Rigid, unyielding, workaholic
Heart:	Low Self Esteem	Excessive Pride and Jealousy
High Heart:	Unable to love self	Narcissism
Throat:	Reserved, stubborn	Boisterous, always "right"
Ajna:	Doubt and fear	Lack of patience
Crown:	Lack of identity	Attention seeking
Soul Star:	Spacey	Reflects ego to world
Tao:	Lack of Oneness	"Homesick" for other world
Interdimensional:	Fear of the unknown	Out of Body excessively

REIKI IRO TERASU
REIKI COLOR ILLUMINATION CHART
Transformational Reiki

CHAKRA	BALANCED	KYO	JITSU
Root:	YES___NO___	Red _____	Green _____
Sacral:	YES___NO___	Orange_____	Blue _____
Solar Plexus:	YES___NO___	Yellow _____	Violet _____
Leydes:	YES___NO___	Saffron _____	Blue-Violet ___
Heart:	YES___NO___	Green _____	Red _____
High Heart:	YES___NO___	Turquoise ___	Red-Orange__
Throat:	YES___NO___	Blue _____	Orange _____
Third Eye:	YES___NO___	Indigo _____	Yellow-Orange___
Crown:	YES___NO___	Violet _____	Yellow _____
Soul Star:	YES___NO___	Silver _____	Met. Black ___
Tao:	YES___NO___	Gold _____	Ultraviolet ___
Inter-dimensional:	YES___NO____	White_____	Black _____

TECHNIQUES TO CHECK BALANCE:

PENDULUM: Your client should lie flat on the Reiki Table or floor. (No pillows.) Utilizing the Tao Pendulum Chart on the next page, place the three inch chart directly upon each chakra to be checked. The Crown, Soul Star, Tao, and Interdimensional Chakras are checked in listed order above the Crown. You speak the name of each chakra three times. In the case of the Root Center, the Tao Pendulum Chart may be placed between the legs near the knees. You then ask: "Is this chakra balanced?" Mark the page with "Yes" or "No." If the answer is no, you must determine if the chakra is Kyo or Jitsu. Say, "Is this chakra Kyo?" (Wait for pendulum to answer.) "Is this chakra Jitsu?" (Wait for pendulum to answer.) Continue through all twelve of the Interdimensional Chakras. Then make the appropriate color application of your choice. (Colored fabric or paper triangles, Stones, Visualization, Aura Soma, Ingesting Colored Infused Water, etc.) A NOTE ABOUT BLACK: If the pendulum answers "NO" to both Kyo and Jitsu, but is unbalanced, perhaps the chakra needs "grounding"...ask, "Does this chakra need Black?" Black contains all colors, just as white does. Black stones like Hematite are well known for their grounding capabilities. Give Reiki Treatment as usual focusing special attention (with symbols if you'd like) upon these chakra centers.

MUSCLE TESTING: Your client is standing. With their arm extended, ask that they give you a "Yes" answer as you apply minimal pressure to the forearm near the wrist. Then ask them to give you a "No." (They should be strong on the yes, and not strong on the "No." If not, ask that they cross their ankles and then their wrists, fingers entwined at chest. Stand that way for one to three minutes to balance. Release and then repeat yes and no questions.) Follow the Reiki Iro Terasu chart listed above. Ask, "Is this chakra balanced?" Mark "Yes" or "No." If "No," muscle test for Kyo and Jitsu. It is best if you can actually have them hold the three inch color triangle at the chakra test site. (For Crown, Soul Star, Tao, and Interdimensional Chakras, they hold color left hand up near forehead.)

PROFILE OF MY DIVINE SELF
A SELF PORTRAIT

ARE YOU A MYSTERY TO YOURSELF? HOW WOULD YOU DESCRIBE YOURSELF TO THE DIVINE PRESENCE?

l.) I AM_____. (Your dominant emotional state.)

2.) I AM_____. (Your dominant mental state.)

3.) I AM_____.(Your dominant spiritual state.)

4.) I AM_____. (Your dominant physical state.)

5.) If I had to describe yourself to someone who had never met you, what would you say?

_____

6.) What colors do you wear?_____What colors make you happy?_____? What color is your soul?_____ (guess)

7.) Are you happy with your life? Why or why not?

_____

8.) Are you living your soul's purpose? Why or why not?

_____

9.) What does your Higher Self look like?

_____

10.) Who (or what) is the presence of the Divine in your life? What do they look like?

_____

11.) Do you consider yourself to be free? Why or why not.

_____

13.) If you could live your life over, what would you change?_____

_____

14.) Do you honestly and unconditionally love yourself?_____

WRITE POSITIVE AFFIRMATIONS FOR EACH APPROPRIATE ANSWER BEGINNING WITH THE WORDS, "I AM." (YOU MAY REFER TO AFFIRMATIONS AS EXAMPLES ON PAGE 13.)

SADDHA REIKI TREATMENT

TRANSFORMATIONAL REIKI TREATMENT FROM THE ANCIENT MASTERS

In Pali, the language of the original Buddhist texts, the word for faith is "Saddha," which translates to: "That which you place your heart upon." It is considered the "gateway" to all good things. This Transformational Reiki treatment is an energy infusion, a Reiki Treatment, that occurs as we invite in the Ancient Healing Masters. Please remember that these Healing Masters will not interfere in your life in any way until requested...they will not pass through the gates of compassion uninvited.

Prepare yourself for a Transformational Reiki experience. The treatment from the Ancient Masters may be accepted on a Reiki Table, in bed, on the floor, or in a sitting meditation position. If you are positioned for a sitting meditation, I suggest the Dhyani mudra where the back of the right hand rests on the upturned palm of the left hand, thumb tips touching. This activates a core of central energy up through the three major meridians of the body: the Ida, which is lunar or cool energy, Pingala, solar or heat energy, which begins at the left of the root chakra and ends at the left nostril, and the Sushumna that follows the spine from the base to the top of the head. Where these meridians intersect in six locations along the spinal column, the major axis chakras are formed. The last major chakra is formed at the connection to the brain, which creates the Crown Chakra. So the process is the upward movement of core energy through the Ida, the Pingala, and the Sushamna, and the subtle energy movement outward through the major axis chakras, outward through the crown, and downward and out through the Root Center.

Put yourself into a meditative state with "So Hum Breathing," or you may instead choose to chant the "Om" or "Aum." Wayne Dwyer also suggests that you may chant the "Ahhh..."

sound, which is the same vowel sound inherent in all spoken names of Infinite Being. (God, Yahweh, Jehovah, Brahman, Shiva, Gansesha, Rama, Allah, Krishna, Kali, etc.) Draw the sound and the vibration into your Tan Tien, the central fire located at the Solar Plexus Center. Feel the fire, the golden-yellow, expand upward and outward, through your three central meridians and your Axis and Crown Chakras. (You may also first breathe in gold energy from the Tao Center down into the Root Center, grounding yourself and the higher energies into the Earth.) Breathe the gold from the Tao into each Interdimensional Chakras: the red of the Root, the orange of the Sacral, the yellow of the Solar Plexus, the saffron of the Leydes (pronounced "Li-den," thus named for a doctor in Holland...as phonetically spelled by Edgar Cayce to his secretary Gladys Davis), the emerald green of the Heart Center, the turquoise of the High Heart Center, the blue of the Throat, the indigo of the Ajna (Third Eye), the violet of the Crown Center, the silver of the soul star, and the gold (with the gold) of the Tao Center. As the golden energy expands outward and upward, feel yourself moving to higher levels of vibrational frequency. You may also see, sense, and feel yourself moving up the eleven golden steps to the Tao, the Eleventh Plane of Higher Energies, the Unisonium. At this Higher Level, request that the Ancient Healing Masters share Their healing energies from the Highest Light with you, if it is in Divine Order and for the Highest Good. Relax and allow the energies to flow to all aspects of your Be-ing for as long as is appropriate. Give thanks and return slowly, back down the eleven steps, from eleven to one. Experiences vary with each individual. I have had people relate to me that they feel "spirit hands" upon their physical body. Others experienced a blissful sense of floating in a white void with luminous colors swirling around them.

SADDHA ABSENTIA TREATMENT

Consider using the Transformational Saddha method for Absentia Healing. Leave all that you do In Divine Order, for the Highest Good. Bring a healee who is not physically with you, or a situation, into the Transformation Space, the Unisonium, for a Saddha Treatment. It is best, in this case, if you notify the healee to set aside fifteen minutes at an appointed time (be mindful of time differences where applicable) for the Transformational Saddha Treatment. Ask them to share in the meditative process by breathing in a healing color (which you may determine ahead of time through Absentia Reiki Iro Terasu), chanting, or by "So Hum Breathing" during the healing process. If you use any technique, such as "So Hum Breathing," to enhance their experience, be certain to explain the significance of doing so with them. It is important that the healee be in a place of comfort where they will not be disturbed for the fifteen minutes of the healing process.

Ask for guidance from their Interdimensional Guides, (and your Guides as well) or any Healing Masters from the Highest Light to assist in this process. Draw the Power Symbol, the Symbol for Absentia Healing, and the Mental Symbol, which some call appropriately the Symbol for Universal Consciousness. (You may also choose to add symbols that you feel are suitable.) At the appropriate time, enter the meditative state through "So Hum Breathing" or chanting a mantra. Follow all procedures previously outlined in the Saddha Reiki Treatment. At the Unisonium, feel and sense the Interdimensional connection to the healee as a golden Light around them, as well as the Ancient Healing Masters and Interdimensional Guides. Sense their presence at the Eleventh Plane, the Unisonium, with you. Be a part of the healing process if you want, as you visualize yourself and the other Ancient Masters sharing Reiki with the healee. Perhaps you will not see the Ancient Masters or the Interdimensional Guides, but sense Their presence or perceive Light, colors, or sound in the process. Perhaps you will receive further guidance to assist or illuminate the healing process. Feel the root cause of the dis-ease being revealed (illuminated) and then dissolved into the Unisonium Field. Remain in the Unisonium with the healee for about fifteen minutes or until you feel the process is complete. Then I generally say a word of thanks to all who assisted in the process, as well as the request: "as Above, so Below, may the healing continue," but you may choose to close the Absentia Treatment in your own traditional manner.

It is also nice to follow up on the Absentia Treatment by calling the healee if it is possible, and to share any positive feelings, affirmations, or words that can assist in furthering the healing process.

TRANSFORMATIONAL REIKI PROCEDURES

As you learn the Transformational tools that you can utilize in Reiki, you may wish to ask your clients if they would like for you to utilize Traditional Reiki or Transformational Reiki in their treatment. I believe that if you use anything other that Traditional Reiki, you should inform your client prior to using any other integrative techniques that what you are offering is not generally part of a Reiki treatment. That way, if they receive Reiki from another practitioner later on, they will not be confused or disappointed.

Before I begin a treatment with a client, especially if it is their first Reiki treatment, I explain the Traditional Reiki procedures and hand placements. I then mention, if I feel that it is appropriate to their particular situation, that I can also...

1.) Check and balance their chakras with color (or stone healing)applications.
2.) Use guided visualization (Trans-Reiki™) to enhance their experience.
   A.) For stress release.
   B.) For releasing energies (Soul or energy clearing.)
   C.) To assist them in contacting their Inner Child, Guides, or Higher Self.

D.) To create a tape for healing that they can listen to daily for healing.
E.) To interact (communicate) with the body itself for direction and healing.
F.) To recognize and release past-life patterns that may be stored in the body.
G.) To speak positive affirmations (to each Body or chakra).
H.) To bring positive healing color into the body.
I.) To prepare them for medical procedures should they choose that path.
J.) To transform negative though patterns
3.) Use directive music, sound, or chanting for particular healing potential.
4.) Utilize Aromatology, Reflexology, Shiatsu, Massage techniques, Breathing, etc.
5.) Use Transformational Hand Placements to balance chakras and energy.

TRANSFORMATIONAL TECHNIQUES AND HAND POSITIONS

Assist client onto table. Sweep their Body. Withhold pillows until chakras are checked.

Check Chakras with <u>Reiki Iro Chart</u>: Apply color corrections. Add pillows and blanket as needed.
Color Breathing: Ask the client to take three deep breaths, breathe in white (or the appropriate color) and exhale any stress. (Stress is other people's energy that we have collected, and generally it is a "Jitsu" response to excess negative energy.)
Draw appropriate symbols, connect to Trans-Guides.
Move to the Unisonium or field of Higher Vibrational Energy, Harmonize breath.
Hand Placements: Simple form. Hold 3-5 minutes each. Visualize color needed.

Transformational Hand Positions
Body Front

1.) Sweep 3 times. Begin with symbols. Then mudra hand meditation.
2.) Hands each side of head (Crown)
3.) Third eye and right side of head
4.) Throat/Crown
5.) Heart/solar plexus
6.) First Hand/Gateway position
7.) Liver/Abdomen (Same side)
8.) Second Hand/gateway position
9.) Sacral/abdomen (Other side)
10.) Thighs (one hand on each)
11.) First knee (Cup hands)
12.) First Knee/ bottom of same foot
13.) Ankles (both)
14.) Second knee /bottom of same foot
15.) Second knee (cup hands around)
16.) Hand on thigh, sweep body 3 times

Body back

1.) Sweep 3 times. Begin with symbols.
2.) Back of occiput and neck (nurture ki at occiput)
3.) Trans-Point stress hold (Do both shoulders)
4.) Sacrum and mid-back between shoulders
5.) Kidneys/adrenals (both) Fingertips toward head each side
6.) Side of upper thighs (both)
7.) Back of upper thighs (optional)
8.) Nurture ki at back of knees
9.) Back of knee and sacrum (both)
10.) Back of calf (both)
11.) Bottoms of foot (both)
12.) Hand on thigh, sweep three times
13.) Seal up spine
14.) Infinity sweep and touch top of head
15.) Optional: circulate ki in head at governing vessel

TRANSFORMATION CLIENT INSTRUCTIONS

ILLUMINATING STORED EMOTIONS

1.) <u>CROWN:</u> TAKE THREE SLOW, DEEP BREATHS AND LET GO OF ALL OF YOUR THOUGHTS. RELAX.

2.) <u>THIRD EYE:</u> SENSE AND FEEL A RADIANT, HEALING ENERGY JUST ABOVE YOUR HEAD.

3.) <u>THROAT/CROWN:</u> FEEL YOUR BODY DRAW THAT HEALING ENERGY DOWN WHERE IT NEEDS TO GO.

4.) <u>HEART/SOLAR PLEXUS:</u> SENSE AND FEEL THAT GOLDEN ENERGY RADIATING THROUGH EACH CELL.

5.) <u>FIRST HAND/GATEWAY:</u> SENSE DEEP IN YOUR BODY ANY FEELINGS THAT ARE IN NEED OF HEALING.

HEALING STORED EMOTIONS

6.) <u>SECOND HAND/GATEWAY:</u> WHERE DID YOU STORE THOSE FEELINGS? (IF POSSIBLE HAVE THEM PLACE THEIR HANDS THERE.)

7.) WHAT DO YOU NEED TO SAY TO THAT EMOTION OR WHATEVER CAUSED IT?

8.) BREATHE THAT GOLDEN LIGHT DEEP INTO THAT PLACE AND EXHALE, LETTING GO.

9.) BREATHE IN VIOLET LIGHT TO FILL THAT SPACE. FEEL HOW LIGHT YOU FEEL.

TRANSFORMATIONAL ABSENTIA

You may utilize Transformational Absentia Healing Techniques In Divine Order for the Highest Good to offer healing opportunities for:

I.) Healing your past especially your Inner Child. Find a picture of yourself at a time that you know you need healing. Hold that picture and give that child (you) Reiki, or send it into your past, Absentee. You may also heal situations or events in your past, and draw that healing forward to the present.

2.) Healing your ancestors if it is in Divine Order.

3.) Healing Mother Earth and all Life Forms.

4.) Building a Bridge of Light to connect to those in transition, or those who have completed their transition.

5.) Joining others in creating a network for Absentia Service.

6.) Healing those places on your own body that you cannot reach.

7.) Sending Reiki to raise the consciousness of humanity.

8.) Releasing old energy patterns (karma) with yourself or others. Our "Soulmates" are oftentimes a result of Karma rather than a matter of the heart.

Chorten

REIKI TRANS-POINTS

Trans-Points 1: AVIDYA. "Avidya" is ignorance or forgetfulness that causes errors to occur in life. Specifically, it refers to three facts that we are ignorant or forget: 1.) That we are first of all Spirit Beings rather than just physical, a spirit that is a part of reality not apart from it. 2.) We confuse the Self with the not-self. 3.) We mistake the fleeting as the eternal. I feel that these energies create great stress and suffering in our lives.

Located (two points) on the back just off each side of the shoulder blades in the upper quadrant of the back, by the Small Intestine Meridian. (See diagram) Press firmly these two points on the back of your client either simultaneously or individually with your Heart Finger (Where the Heart Energy Meridian begins, between the index finger and the ring finger). This will aid in releasing stress. The other fingers and the palms of the hands continue to channel Reiki energy as well. The focused energy and pressure through these Trans-Points can be intense, so it is important that the client communicate with you. You may also add to this procedure any Symbols, Kotama Scripts, or the Unisonium Technique. Be aware that Past-life memories may be stored at Trans-Points 1. The Practitioner may assist in healing these memories and releasing them. It works especially well in dealing with most karmic weight issues including Anorexia and Bulimia.

Trans-Hold 1: AVIDYA HOLD: (Refer to Photograph) Performed first on one side of the body, then the other. I prefer to begin on the left side of the client (their Yin side) as they lie face down upon the table. Your left hand grips firmly but gently, the muscle in the center that connects the neck to the shoulder joint. Your right hand rests just below it, giving Reiki, on the right outside edge of the shoulder blade. You press Trans-Point 1 with your Heart Finger and hold for ten seconds. Release. Repeat two more times. Sweep three times. Apply Reiki there for one to three minutes without moving your hands; there is no pressure, no gripping. Repeat everything on the right side (Yang side) of the body. This Hold is also effective for a grieving or broken heart. An affirmation that might prove beneficial in such a case is: "Life continues, love never ends."

Self Treatment Trans-Point 1. Release: I like to share this release with clients who have stress or Chronic Fatigue, and often use it myself. Right hand grips large muscle between neck and shoulder blade on the left side. Maintain grip, but pull hand forward adding pressure. "Row" slowly ten times backward with left arm bent at elbow, bring the elbow as high as possible with each circular motion. Repeat with other arm.

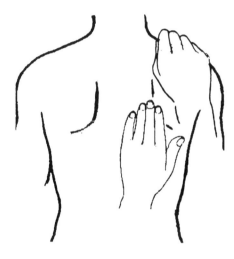

Back of Body

SHAMA: Mind Calming or Still Point Hold: One might use the "Murccha" or mind-quieting breath with this hold. The purpose is to assist the client in focusing energy and intention inward. Heart Finger of Practitioner's right hand is placed gently but firmly on the Governing Vessel at the Ajna Center between the brows. Palm of right hand rests on client's right temple. Left Heart Finger is placed gently but firmly on on the Governing Vessel at the back of the head between the occiput ridges. (It is suggested in some cultures that the soul enters the body at this location.) Please be mindful never to lift the head when a client is lying on their back! Slide the hand beneath the neck with little commotion, or tilt the head to the side. You might also ask the client to turn their head for you. This hold is powerful to ease circular arguments in a depressed client, but can also still someone who talks too much rather ran listening to the Noble Silence of their own body. It stills the Mental Body and creates a clearer pathway for the soul to communicate. If you utilize this hold on yourself, by closing your eyes and looking upward at the Crown Center for a few moments from the inside of your head, you can enhance the reception of messages from your Higher Self.

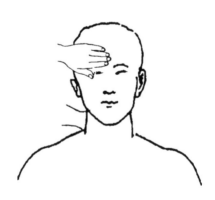

Trans-Point 2: BHAKTI POINT. Bhakti means love or devotion. It is a path to communicate with your Higher Self (Your Transformed Self) or God. The experiences stored in this Point are highly charged emotions. Healing this Trans-Point may lead to a understanding of higher love called "para-bhakti."

Client is facing up on the table, or standing. This Point is located on the Conception Vessel beneath the pit of the throat, one finger width below the junction of the two collar bones. (Thymus) Place the Heart Finger on Trans-Point 2. If You are familiar with this person, or if you have permission, allow the palm of your right hand to rest on the sternum. If not, allow the palm to float above the sternum while holding this point with the Heart Finger. Left hand rests gently, barely touching, perpendicular to the right hand, going across the base of the throat area or a bit lower at the High Heart. The purpose of this hold is twofold: 1.) It releases emotionally charged energies trapped in the High-Heart and Throat area, and 2.) It boosts the immune system in the case of dis-ease.

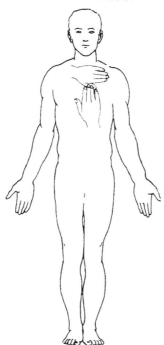

Trans-Point 3: BRAHMA or SURYA POINT. The Place of Pre-natal and infant pain. The "Brahma-Nadi" means "river of God," and refers to the Sushumna Channel, or the central astral channel between the Ida and the Pingala. These channels coil around each other, and where they create a braid or intersect, each of the six (seven, if you count the crown, which has no physical connection) major, central axis chakras is born.

This point is also located on the Conception Vessel just one inch above the naval. Place Heart Finger on Point 3, with slight pressure, while palm of that same hand rests on Leydes Center. Other hand rests above it on the Solar Plexus Center. (This hand later moves to High Heart, for Trans-Hold 3 or "Brahma Hold") As you hold this Point, ask your client to move the focus of all emotions to that Point, and feel, sense, and know that they are able to get in touch with very old emotional pain or suffering. Ask them to tell you what they feel, or you, as the practitioner may wish to use Kotama Script 3 or Rebirthing Script with the Brahma Hold. "The Ceremony of Birthrite Tea" later in the book, is also suggested.

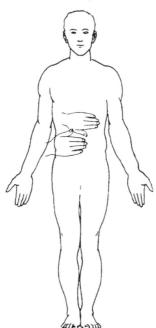

Trans-Point 4: DAHARA. This point links the mind, body, and the Transformational Self within the Anahata (Heart) Center. Located just below the sternum on the Conception Vessel. Heart Finger presses gently on Dahara point while same hand is allowed to rest vertical on the Solar Plexus. Other hand is on the Heart Center. The purpose of igniting this Point is to create greater "space" in the Heart Chakra, and sometimes is alleviates emotional congestion. You might have client breathe in green healing Light as you press the Dahara, and release as they exhale. Three, nine, or twelve breathes are suggested for the Dahara Clearing.

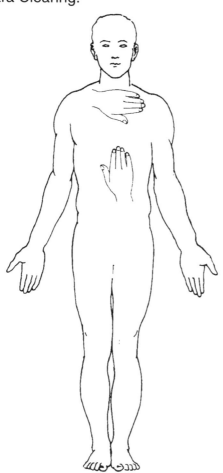

Trans-Point 5: SHANTI: On the top of the head Governing Vessel # 20 in combination with "Yin Tang," a point in the center of the Third Eye located between the eye brows. One must be mindful in using this hold, for if too much pressure is used, or if it is over-stimulated, a headache may result. Otherwise, it is a powerful connection that can be utilized in self treatment or meditation. In such a case, you might enhance the energies by chanting "OM" or "Shanti" (which means "peace"). Another powerful mantra is: "OM, shanti, shanti, shantih." This translates into: "May the physical, mental, and causal universe be in equilibrium." The purpose of the Shanti hold is to harmonize and balance all centers, extremely beneficial in assisting depression or anxiety.

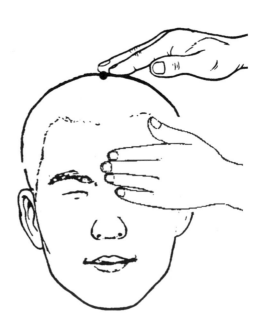

Trans-Points 6: CHITTA. Chitta means lower mind or mind stuff. It is the storage place of all correct and incorrect information. We must first master this section of the mind.

Combined light pressure of Practitioner's Heart fingers on two points, called "Yin Tang" and "Tai Yang." Thumb may be used on second "Tai Yang" point, or even on the "Yin Tang." "Yin Tang" is located exact center between eyebrows, the heart of the Third Eye Chakra, "Tai Yang" is located at the outside of the eyebrow at the hollow of the temple. Dissolves negative thoughtforms or inappropriate messages and opens the Mental Body. May use the Kotama Script 2 for Mental Healing, or a prearranged affirmation. The Mental Symbol is extremely useful with this process.

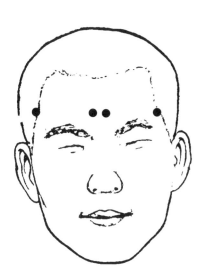

Trans-Point 7: TALAS: Talas is located in the thigh bone area, and connects symbolically to the lower nether regions. It is located on the Gallbladder Channel, on the outside of the thigh, nearly one vertical hand length down from the hipbone. Press gently but firmly both Talas points (one on each leg) with Heart Finger simultaneously. The purpose of this hold is to diffuse and liberate Ki to increase strength in the physical body. The legs may jump in response to the release of Ki.

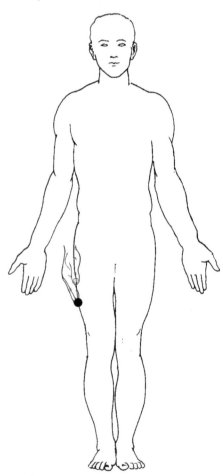

Trans-Point 8: DHARMA. Dharma is located on each arm just above the elbow, on the center outside of the arm. Press only one Dharma Point at a time. If that point is sensitive, it can mean "too many burdens." It can also mean that we try too hard to please a significant other (or parent). If the right arm is sensitive, our "Dharma" issues are with a male, on the left, female.

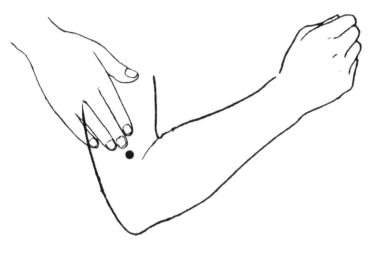

TRANSFORMATIONAL REIKI TREATMENT APPLICATIONS

One of the great "Mysteries" for most practitioners is how to apply Reiki to specific challenges, healing opportunities, or major dis-eases. I am including this chapter only on the basis of my own personal healing work. It is by no means a complete course of action, and it is my hope that you research each particular dis-ease, as these applications, especially concerning herbs, are of a general nature, a place to begin.

Do full body Self-treatment daily, and then add to the process these specific healing opportunities. Utilize symbols as you feel necessary. Please consider Reiki Iro Color Treatments in conjunction with each treatment. The Chakras treated may be Jitsu (excess) or Kyo (deficient). I also find it useful to invoke the symbol of "Kotama" as well and your own or the following affirmation:

> "Kotama, Kotama, Kotama may these words spoken illuminate and guide my Higher Self on the Path to healing. May I serve as a clear channel for the Highest Light, and may all of the Highest Light Who wish to be present with me be here and present with me now. I extend gratitude and love for their Divine Presence. May I, with Divine assistance reawaken in my body the original intent and natal blueprint for health and wellbeing, restore joy and peace to all bodies. As Above, so below, may the healing continue..."

I always invite the flame of a white candle during any type of Reiki Treatment. As I light it, I say to myself: "I ignite the healing flame (of Buddha Christ, or the Ancient Healing Masters) within me." **I might suggest the following applications:**

Acne: Liver "T" hand placements (R.H. Vertical on right side, and L.H. Horizontal fingers touching R.H.), Third Eye (Pituitary), Intestines. **Herbal Etc:** Zinc, Acidophilus, Omega 3 Flax Oil, Beta Carotene (25,000 IU 2X daily), B Complex, Vitamin C, Essiac or Milk Thistle for the liver. Topical applications of: Tea Tree Essential Oil, or Castor Oil warmed in microwave on wet Echinacea Tea bag; reheat and apply three times to blemishes. Dandelion Root, Burdock Root, Yellow Dock Root to cleanse the blood and liver. **Stones:** Wear or carry Blood Stone. **Affirm:** I release all negativity and anger and embrace only positive thoughts and emotions.

Addictions: There may be may reasons for addictions, but I believe that three are most obvious. I suggest ten minutes for each specified Chakra. 1.) Lack of self-love: hand placements on the High Heart Center, Root Center, and Spleen (Sacral) Center. 2.) Control issues with self or others: hand placements on the Solar Plexus, then the Throat. 3.) Depression or a death wish: Occipital ridge at back of head and High Heart Chakra simultaneously; then Root Center Solar Plexus simultaneously. (See also Kotama Script for "Releasing Addictions From the Spiritual Body.") **Herbal Etc:** Kava-Kava, CoQ10, Selenium, Potassium, and Trace Minerals for all. The body must be cleansed of addictive toxins and Candida. Probiotics and Pau D'arco tea assist for alcohol or food addictions. See also Detox Bath (in Arthritis). **Stones:** Wear or carry Rose Quartz or Pink Tourmaline for self love.

Affirm: I understand my soul's purpose is to love and accept myself and all that I am. I am free of all negative energy and allow only positive energy into my thoughts, aura, and body.

Age Reversal: Hand placements on Leydes Center simultaneously for ten minutes. Then Third Eye (LH) and liver (RH). **Herbal Etc:** Antioxidents, Ginkgo Biloba, Vitamin E. Also "The Five Tibetan Rites" of Rejuvenation. (Explained in this book, or you may call Mind Rivers 815-732-7150 for the professional

video available at $29.95) Men: Hawthorne, Saw Palmetto, and chromium/selenium. Women: Vitex, Hawthorne, and if needed, Wild Yam.
 Affirm: I am my optimal age, and all bodies reflect that age. I feel and look great.

A.I.D.S. (Refer to chapter on A.I.D.S. by Master Hamilton in my book, Reiki Beyond the Usui System) Immune "T" position on sternum/High Heart, as well as entire length of spine. Solar Plexus, Spleen Center Simultaneously, as well as the liver. **Herbal Etc:** I suggest the programs listed in Hulda Clark's book, The Cure for H.I.V. **Stones:** Wear or carry Pink Tourmaline or Rose Quartz.
Affirm: All sacred Bodies respond to the record of my original blueprint. I am healthy, happy, whole, and well. I ordain my body to respond to the image of perfect health. (Optional) I love, accept, and forgive myself and all others, and release for healing any active, dormant, or potential karma that exists, in Divine Order.

Anger: Place one hand on the liver and the other on the Solar Plexus Center. Anger is related to an energy of the past, as we must have a reference for anger. The Heart and High Heart may also need attention for wounds related to childhood that may be creating anger. **Herbal Etc:** Milk Thistle, Kava-Kava, or St. John's Wort. Epsom Salts Detox. (See Arthritis) Avoid all caffeine or toxic substances. **Stones:** Wear or carry Green Tourmaline.
Affirm: I am not the energy of anger. For all past, present, and future, I forgive and release any energy or energies that are not serving my Highest Good. Within and without, I release, and from all Bodies, thought forms, words, and deeds, I release and heal. (Optional: "Kadoish, Kadoish, Kadoish, Adonai Tsebayoth", or nothing of darkness can stand in the Light.)

Anorexia Nervosa: Solar Plexus, then High Heart, then both.

Herbal Etc: Zinc, Ener B (B12 Nasal), Acidophilus, Nettles or Iron supplementation, Angelica Tea **Stones:** Wear or carry citrine.

Affirm: I am free and in control of my all aspects of my life. I forgive and release myself and all others.

Arthritis: Reach both hands around to back at kidneys for ten minutes. Sweep as best you can. Press and hold with Heart Finger the area of the foot at the middle just below the ball of the foot (Kidney Point 1 in accupressure) for three minutes. Arthritis detox bath: drink a cup of Yarrow tea, which acts as a diaphoretic. Fill a bathtub with very warm water in which is dissolved 2 cups of Epsom Salt. Soak for fifteen minutes. Leave tub, towel off, then wrap in blankets until sweating ceases in about ten minutes. This is not suggested if you have any hypertension, heart disease, or are expecting a baby. **Herbal Etc:** Trace Minerals, Glucosamine (with Chondroitin, if you are not vegetarian), Aloe Vera Juice, Green Tea or Chlorella, Omega 3 Flax or Borage Oil. **Stones:** Wear or carry Blood Stone and use a compress of the elixer of Blood Stone on the affected areas.

Affirm: I am flexible in all bodies.

If in the hands, make a fist and then cover the hand with other hand for ten minutes. If in the knees or ankles, wrap hands around the joint and hold each for ten minutes.

Affirm: I release the past and others and let go of all fears. I welcome change.

Back: RH horizontal on Seventh Cervical Vertebra. LH vertical on sacrum. You may then apply energy to the length of the spine through the front of the body, visualizing each vertebra receiving energy, or you may choose to work with your spine in Absentia, via the "Thigh Method" or with a surrogate. A photocopy or picture of the spine from an anatomy text could also be used in the Absentia process. I have heard that lower back pain may be caused by financial worry or carrying around other people's burdens. If this is the case, the affirmation would be: I release these (financial, personal, or other person's) burdens.

Herbal Etc: Edgar Cayce's Violet Ray (Available from Heritage Store, Virginia Beach, VA) Yoga "Cobra," if you are able, Detox Bath (See Arthritis), St. John's Wort, Valerian, Borage Oil, Trace Minerals, Vitamins A, B, E, and C. **Stones:** Wear or carry or use a layout of Carnelian on the back.

Affirm: I am flexible and my Will Centers are free of past, limiting energies.

Breathing Challenges: Asthma: If worry or stress motivated, apply hands to the High Heart, Solar Plexus simultaneously. Then High Heart, Heart simultaneously (Steam might assist with symptoms of Asthma or Bronchitis) Bronchitis: Attend to the intestines by placing both hands (simultaneously) vertical three inches each side of the navel. Then vertical close to navel. Then horizontal (simultaneously) above and below the navel. Allergies, lung cancer, or emphysema: Heart, High Heart simultaneously, then the liver and intestines (See arthritis for treating intestines.) **Herbal Etc:** Study the herbal parasite program, liver and kidney cleanse presented in Hulda Clark's book, The Cure For All Diseases. Healing Diet of Paavo Airola (Found in my book Reiki Beyond the Usui System). Most Naturopaths would recommend that all dairy be eliminated from the diet (and perhaps wheat, refined sugar, and yeast if symptoms are severe). Essential Oil of Eucalyptus and or Peppermint. **Stones:** Lay Angelite on the lungs or throat.

Affirm: I honor Prana, the breath of life. My mind releases all judgments, guilt, arguments, and fear. I am free to breathe with ease. If karmic, one might consider the "Invocation to release karma."

Bulimia: Third Eye, Throat simultaneously. High Heart, Solar Plexus simultaneously. Then Solar Plexus. Optional: R.H. horizontal over occiput, L.H. "T's" vertical down spine. **Herbal Etc:** Zinc, Herbal Iron or Nettles, Nasal "Ener B," Vitamin C, Kava Kava, Trace Minerals, Sea Vegetables, Acidophilus. **Stones:** Citrine

Affirm: I sense the fire of Divine Will in my Solar Plexus. I will to be free, powerful, and strong. I trust my own judgments and set my own course in my life. I am in charge.

Cancer: (See chapter in Reiki, Beyond the Usui System) Immune "T" position on sternum (R.H. vertical) and High Heart (L.H. horizontal), May apply hands to cancer or tumor sites directly if you have permission, liver, and hands vertical entire length of spine. "T" at coccyx/sacrum if you have permission to do so. Suggest 4 days of Reiki in a row, rest 2-3 days. 4 days Reiki, rest 2-3 days. Then 2 times a week or more thereafter.

There are many Herbal philosophies concerning cancer. I suggest the programs specified by Dr. Hulda Clark in her book, The Cure for All Cancers. "Essiac" tincture is a formula of Burdock Root, Turkey Rhubarb, and Sheep's Sorrel, and is most often recommended. Antioxidents, Selenium, Aloe Vera, Garlic, Beta Carotene, High Dose of CoQ10, Detox Bath (See Arthritis). Candida Program, Chi Kung daily. **Stones:** Lay Smoky Quartz on the affected area. Raw Ruby.
Affirm: I release judgment, fear, anger, or any emotions that are not serving my Highest Good. Blue Healing Light flows through the channels of by body, bathing each cell with health, peace, and harmony. Disharmony or dis-ease flows out through my system of elimination. I recall and restore my original health and well-being. I choose to be healthy, strong, and well, and my body reflects this choice.

Candida: Reiki the liver, stomach, and abdomen. Focus energy in index fingers and place tips of fingers into each ear. Forehead and back of head simultaneously. I suggest the program in William Crook's books, The Yeast Connection. I feel three things about Candida: 1.) It is a precursor to Cancer, and 2.) It takes six months or more to control it. Once you have it, you must always watch for symptoms. 3.) It is a major problem in the United States because of widespread use of antibiotics and our diets which include too much sugar, yeast, and alcohol. There is often a link with Candida and alcoholism and weight challenges. **Herbs Etc:** (Along with Dr. Crook's programs) Pau D'Arco tincture 3X daily before meals. Ear Candle three or more times a week if Candida is systemic. Avoid dairy, sugar, and yeast products. Acidophilus and Bifidus three times a day. Leg lifts, Yoga, or Chi Kung, plus deep breathing, to oxygenate body. Lavender Essential Oil for Yeast Infections. If depressed, St. John's Wort. NOTE: If you do not follow the Crook regimen: Hanna Kroeger's "Cantita, Foon Goos 2, and Stay Sober." Call us for "Harmony" Formula.

Affirm: All cravings are for health and exercise. I allow only food that nourishes me into my body. I nurture and honor myself and feel good when I follow my program. I no longer allow other energies to dictate my diet or my life.

Carpal Tunnel Syndrome: Hold wrists simultaneously or one at a time, for ten minutes, three times a day. Optional: liver and kidneys. **Herbs Etc:** Vitamin C, 300mg of B6 daily for 90days.
Stones: Wear or lay Raw Ruby on the wrist.
Affirm: I release, bend, and allow my hands to be free of energy bondage.

Cold, Viruses: Immune "T." Vertical length of spine and sacrum.
Herbs Etc: Zinc, Echinacea, Oregon Grape tincture.
Affirm: I am free of negative thoughts, negative energy, and negative advertisements. I release the need to be ill in order to rest. I listen to my body, and it allows me to know when I need to rest. My immune system is strong, I breathe deeply, drawing in healing energy and blue healing color. All systems are clear.

Death and Dying: According to Pandit Rajmani Tigunait, "Not finding your Self is called death, and finding your Self is immortality." We are all immortal, we just change physical bodies when it is appropriate. Focus on the Crown, Heart, and Solar Plexus. Yogis believe that the evolved soul exits the body through the Solar Plexus. Remember that all healing is not of a physical nature. Look up at the Light. **Herbs Etc**: For purification and preparation according to your beliefs. Lavender essential oil, Sandalwood essential oil on the temples, navel, and bottoms of feet. **Stones:** Use a layout of White Quartz around the body.

Affirm: Whatever serves the Highest Good. I forgive and release all and everyone, including myself. I choose to remember. (May chant "OM," or as Mahatma Gandhi did speak the name of your God, or invoke Masters.)

Depression: Sweep body front and back (as best you can) three times. Begin with Crown Center, then Third Eye and Occiput simultaneously. Liver: open thumb away from right hand. Slide four fingers of left hand into the space between index finger and thumb. Place both hands connected in this fashion onto the liver. Hand placements on intestines are optional. (See also "Shanti" Trans-point procedure.) **Herbs Etc**: St. John's Wort and Glutamine. Drink more water, obtain more oxygen in the system through exercise or walking and deep breathing (see Pranayama Color Breathing), more sunlight or full spectrum lighting (especially in the winter), avoid caffeine. **Stone:** Sunstone

Affirm: I release all energy that is not serving my Highest Good. I nurture the seeds of joy and freedom in my Heart Center. I realize the great opportunities that life offers. (Breathe in violet Light.)

Diabetes: Sweep liver and pancreas area of body. (Right side just beneath the ribcage.) Right hand assumes vertical position, pointing down, while left hand is perpendicular and touches the middle joint of the index finger. The pancreas is the "joyometer" of the body; it is said that one must be happy for the pancreas to function properly. For this reason, I also suggest the treatment of the High Heart Chakra, which is self-love. Treat then sweep three times. **Herbal Etc:** Aloe Vera Juice, Gymema sylvestre before meals, Magnesium/potassium, Pau D'Arco extract, garlic, Bilberry, and Astragalus. May use stevia herb (liquid or dry form) instead of sugar. Candida or HuldaClark program. Exercise such as Yoga or Chi Kung. Walking.

Affirm: I create balance, harmony, and joy in all of my bodies past, present, and future.

Ears: Cup palms over ears. Focus energy into the index or heart finger of each hand and place finger in each ear. Visualize a specific color (such as green) that is needed as a laser light clearing the ears. **Herbs Etc:** Chronic ear infections may be caused by allergies to dairy or wheat. In such cases, you may wish to apply energy to the intestines. Herb: Goldenseal. If ears are not infected, they may be congested with Candida yeast. You might consider ear candles two to three times a week to remove yeast, if ears are not infected.

Affirm: I listen deeply and desire to hear the world around me. I have the ability to transmute sounds and words into positive energy.

Eyes: Sweep three times. Place palm of hands over closed eyes for ten minutes. Sweep three times. Reach both hands around to back at kidneys for ten minutes. Sweep as best you can. **Herbs Etc:** Press and hold with Heart Finger the area of the foot at the middle just below the ball of the foot (Kidney Point 1 in accupressure) for three minutes. Bilberry, Ginkgo Biloba, Vitamin E, Zinc, Eyebright. Support the kidney and liver with appropriate herbs.

Affirm: I have clear perceptions and see things as they really are, free of fear.

Fear: In The Tradition of the Himalayan Masters (by Pandit Rajmani Tigunait) the great sage Sanatkumara states: "There are two forms of fear--the fear of not having enough to maintain yourself and the fear of being consumed by the objects you possess. " (p. 29) "Fear springs from duality. With the knowledge of non-dual truth, one attains immortality." (p. 17) Fear is a threatening of the subconscious with an unrealized energy. Hand applications include the upper Kidneys (for adrenal stress) Root Center (survival threatened) and the Throat Center (fear of Truth or speaking Truth) simultaneously. May also choose the Solar Plexus (to clarify power) and Spleen (to release insecurity and empower identity). **Herbs Etc:** Bach Flower Rescue Remedy, Calcium with Borion, Skullcap, Valerian, Magnesium, Tyrosine, Ener B nasal, Lavender Essential Oil, Deep Breathing, Tai Chi exercises.

Affirm: I am safe and peaceful, alive and well. The Universe protects and provides for my Highest Good.

Fibroids: In breast: Reiki Liver and fibroid site simultaneously. LH Third Eye and RH Right ovary/uterus; then RH Third Eye and LH Left ovary/uterus. Uterus: Spleen (horizontal) and Root (vertical) simultaneously in a "T" formation. (May attend to all reproductive organs physically, if they are present still, or etherically. Your body still recognizes their presence even if they have been surgically removed.) **Herbs Etc:** Fasting under supervision, see Hulda Clark's book, A Cure for All Diseases, Antioxidents, Omega 3 oils, Vitex, Edgar Cayce's Atomadine. Candida Program. **Stone:** Moonstone

Affirm: I release all excess, stored energy in all bodies (and organs) that is not serving my highest good. I release all negative emotional thoughts stored in all bodies, including the (name the reproductive organ) of fear, judgment, jealousy, and lack of self-love.

Headache: (Is generally a symptom of perhaps food allergies or msg repercussions, hormonal or sugar imbalance, stress, a toxic liver, intestinal disturbance such as lack of Acidophilus/Bifidus, Candida, or need for spinal adjustment.) Hold Third Eye and Occiput simultaneously. Breathe in blue and breathe out steam until pressure subsides. If headache pain persists: entire area surrounding navel, concentrating on the liver and intestines. **Herbs Etc:** If you are challenged by headaches on a regular basis, I would change diet, consider drinking more water, and eliminate stress. The herb White Willow Bark or a few drops of lavender oil in warm water may assist. If you are not expecting a baby, and are not challenged by fibroids, three drops of Clary sage essential oil (for hormonal headaches) on the outside of the ankles, and or peppermint oil on the temples (avoid the eyes) may bring immediate relief.

Affirm: I listen to my body as I ask, "What do you need?" I release all fear and supply that need. Breathing in, I am free. Exhale: I create peace and open space in my head.

Insomnia: Solar Plexus and Sacral Center simultaneously.
Herbs Etc: Chamomile, Skullcap, non-animal source of Melatonin. Lavender Essential Oil on the pillow case, or the tip of your nose if you are accustomed to it applied neat.
Affirm: Your personal Mantra or "Om Mani Padme Hum," or I sweep my mind clear of all thoughts. I invoke the soft, white energy of rest to envelope me. I sleep now.

Irritable Bowel or Crohn's: Fear is sometimes stored in the intestines. Place hands on intestines and move in a circular fashion from the liver across to the left side, down the left side, then across and back up to the liver in a counterclockwise fashion. Optional: Root Center to release fear concerning survival, Solar Plexus for control issues. Or Third Eye and High Heart simultaneously for Higher Awareness. **Herbs Etc:** Glutamine, Herbal Pregnenolone. Essential Oil of Lavender to release tension. Hynotherapy. "Harmony " Formula.
Affirm: I create my life free of fear. I know that fear is "false experience appearing real." Energy flows freely through my abdomen and intestines. I choose to be happy.

Marital or Significant Other Conflict or Disharmony: Facing your significant other, place your right hand on their Heart Center, left hand on their Solar Plexus. They place their left hand on your Heart Center and right hand on your Solar Plexus. Close your eyes and remember what you appreciate most about this person. **Herbs Etc:** I suggest the book, Getting the Love You Need, by Harville Hendrix. Communicate and spend time together. Create an herbal "Marriage Tea" to share. Each herb represents a positive emotion you wish to share. Touch, Trust, Talk.

Affirm: I send and accept unconditional love.

Multiple Personality Disorder or Schizophrenia: Third Eye and Liver. Visualize a violet light flowing from the Third Eye to the Liver. **Herbs Etc.:** Kava Kava, Valerian. **Stone:** Pyrite

Affirm: I release any thoughts or energies that are not a part of my original Divine Being.

Psoriasis, Skin: (See "Stress") Apply hands to liver and then kidneys. The skin is the third route of detox for chemicals and toxins. **Herbs Etc:** Hulda Clark's Program, especially the liver and kidney cleanse. **Stone:** Malachite

Affirm: I am calm and clear. I release all fear, anxiety, and insecurity from all Bodies. I bathe my skin in Light. (Visualize an appropriate healing Light color.)

Sinus: Cup palms over sinuses for three to ten minutes. Then, focus energy into tips of fingers. Place little fingers on side of each nose, three fingers press on each eyebrow, thumbs on each earlobe pulling forward. Press to count of ten, release ten. Repeat two more times. May also apply energy to intestines, especially if you feel sinus challenges may be related to dairy or wheat allergies. Avoid dairy. **Herbs Etc:** If chronic, read The Cure for All Diseases by Hulda Clark. Flush sinuses with Neti pot and tinctures (Which have set in hot water for ten minutes to evaporate the alcohol) of: Eyebright, Yerba Manza, Usnea, Echinacea, and Myrrh dissolved in 1/4 tsp of sea salt to 1 C. distilled water, which has been gently boiled Allow to set for ten minutes to evaporate the alcohol. Tincture of Yerba Manza, Echinacea, Myrrh, and Red Root. **Affirm:** My Yin, my Yang are balanced in my breath. All passages are free.

Stress: Solar Plexus and Sacral Center. Leydes Center (each side of the navel). Heart and High Heart simultaneously. Press point midway between neck and shoulder on top of back. (Called Triple Heater or Triple Warmer). Nurture counter-clockwise. For people who do too much or are overwhelmed. **Herbs Etc:** Antioxidents, Licorice, B Complex, Chamomile, Reishi, Bach Flower Rescue Remedy, Kava Kava, Valerian, Deep Breathing practices, Yoga, Chi Kung, or Tai Chi. Meditation. **Stone:** Rose Quartz

Affirm: Choose what is most appropriate: I am a human being, not a human doing. I release other people's energy. I see myself as a magnet, reversing polarities, sending all energy, thoughts, and thought forms where they need to go to their place of Highest Spiritual Development. I feel where I have stored stress. I open the windows in this place. (Take a deep breath in.) I breathe in Light. (Exhale) I am free! (Breathe out stress. You may see or sense this as a dark color).

Soul Loss: Heart and Solar Plexus simultaneously. **Herbs Etc:** Angelica tea, Lavendar Essential Oil. **Stones:** Amythest **Affirm:** In Divine Order, for the Highest Good, (Optional: I request Divine Assistance in this process). I release any energy that is not a part of me. It must now go, go, go. I now call back to me (reclaim) any part of me that I may have lost, given away, or had stolen through any part of my existence in any place, time, or dimension. I welcome this energy with love back to where it needs to go in my body. I anchor my energy back with golden Light. I am worthy of love and wholeness.

Unhappiness: Unhappiness seems to have two root causes: 1.) Inert behavior or 2.) Lack of sense of power or responsibility in one's life. As adults, we cannot blame anyone else for our unhappiness, as we have the power to change or transform our lives. We must want to change things and know that we can. Spleen Center. High Heart, Heart simultaneously. **Herbs Etc:** St. John's Wort or Kava-Kava. Bach Flower Rescue Remedy. Milk Thistle. **Stones:** Pink Tourmaline or RoseQuartz.

Affirm: I am responsible for my own happiness. I take action. I release any energy that is limiting or blocking my happiness, and I invite Light, Joy, and Peace into my Self.

Weight: (See "Addictions" and or "Candida" and apply recommendations there as needed) Work with Solar Plexus and Spleen Center simultaneously, then Third Eye. Your body is an evolutionary process of countless lifetimes. You manifest the body you need to activate and actualize your soul's purpose. However, some souls do not understand that the food of the past few decades has become a technology rather than a sustenance. To that effect, cravings may arise from a lack of vitamins and minerals that are now also missing in our soil. If weight is a Past-life or karmic issue, I suggest the "Invocation to Release Karma." **Stones:** Aquamarine

Affirm: "I forgive myself and all others in relation to negative judgment. My body reflects the process of my soul's evolution and purpose. I ask for illumination and understanding to move to a new level of awareness concerning this image and the nature of my True Self. (Or: I see myself as I really am, my true perception is illuminated. I love and accept myself and all that I was, am, or will be.)

Clark's Rule: Divide 150 by a child's weight to achieve the appropriate herbal dosage; for example, if your child weighs 50 pounds, you divide 150 by 50 and that is 3, so the formula for your child is 1/3 the dose indicated on the bottle.

NATURE'S PROZAC; ST. JOHN'S WORT

The sacred herb, Hypericum, or St. John's Wort as it is commonly called, has an ancient mystical reputation for casting out evil spirits. The Latin name, Hypericum, is derived from the Greek root word that translates literally, "over an apparition:"

"The Latin name Hypericum...is a reference to the belief that the herb was so obnoxious to evil spirits that a whiff of it would cause them to quickly depart the premises. The (common) name St. John's Wort has its origins in Christian folk traditions. One belief held that the red spots appeared on the leaves during the anniversary of St. John's beheading and symbolized his blood." (Brown and Foster, "Phytotherapy, Herbal Medicine Meets Clinical Science," Bastyr University Continuing Professional Education Program, p. 25)

Yet another legend concerning the naming of the herb is that the Knights of St. John of Jerusalem used the plant to treat wounds collected in battle. The insane were also forced to drink infusions of St. John's Wort to drive out the evil spirits within. Bakers added St. John's Wort to their flour to enhance the spiritual quality of their bread. It was the magical blend of the Middle Ages, mysteriously reputed to ward off not only evil spirits, but illness and plague as well:

"The wild St. John's Wort has long been valued as a potent medicinal herb and has a very rich folkloric tradition...Dioscorides, the most famous herbalist of the ancient Greeks, mentions the use of St. John's Wort for sciatica and other nerve problems. So do many of the other ancient Greek healers: Theophratus recommended it for external wounds and cuts; Pliny recommended taking it in wine for poisonous reptiles; and it was included in the materia medica of Galen and Paracelsus. In pre-

Christian religious practices in England, St. John's Wort was used in many of the ceremonies and rituals. Bringing the flowers into the house on mid-summers eve would protect against the evil eye; and sleeping with a sprig of the plant under one's pillow on St. John's Eve would ensure a vision of the Saint and his blessing...the word 'WORT' is an ancient Anglo Saxon word for HERB; the herb was named the herb of St. John."

"As you can see, the tradition of St. John's Wort is rich and varied. Some of these traditions still live on in the hearts of people. I know of many herbalists today who wait until June 24th to pick the herb. And many who hang bundles of it in their homes, in part, I'm sure, in memory of the old ways; but also, because traditions run deep."

"In the last thirty years St. John's Wort has undergone extensive clinical and laboratory testing. Modern research and clinical studies validate the powerful medicinal actions that the early doctors of Greece and Roman espoused. St. John's Wort has powerful nerve regenerative abilities. It also has marked anti-bacterial, anti-viral, and anti-inflammatory properties. Recently, a strong inhibition of the AIDS virus by hypericin and psuedohypericin, two active constituents from St. Johns Wort, was confirmed. Studies are being conducted at the present time to further authenticate this action...Although there has been extensive studies done, there has never been a case involving human toxicity. St. John's Wort has been used for centuries and in modern Europe is included in many over-the-counter and prescription drugs." (Rosemary Gladstar, "The Science and Art of Herbology," p. 36)

The modern day application of Hypericum or St. John's Wort is not so different than it was in ancient times. Recent research into the properties of the herb have revealed that it is an antidepressant "either greater than placebo or equal in action to standard prescription drugs." (J. Holzl, "Constituents and mechanism of action of St. John's Wort," Zeitschrift

Phytother 1993; 14:255-64) St. John's Wort drives away the blues, regardless of whether you choose to call it "evil spirits" as they did in Medieval days of folklore, or depression or stress in the 90's. The energy of darkness is dispelled by the spirit of the plant called Hypericum. "The standardized extract dosage as suggested is generally 0.3% hypericin at a daily dose of 300 mg three times daily." (Brown and Foster, "Phytotherapy, Herbal Medicine Meets Clinical Science, Part II," Bastyr University Continuing Professional Education Program, p. 27)

I discovered the powerful application of St. John's Wort years ago in an effort to aid in the treatment of my own Seasonal Affective Disorder. SAD is the nickname for the effects of lack of sunlight upon the spiritual, emotional, mental, and physical bodies. I found that by taking St. John's Wort at the end of Daylight Saving's Time (fall back) to its reinstatement (spring ahead), I could alleviate many of the symptoms of lack of joy that were as much a part of my winter as the wearing of a coat or sweater. "A recent study has suggested that St. John's Wort extract may also be helpful in the management of seasonal affective disorder. A study of 20 SAD patients (13 women and 7 men) gave each patient 900 mg of St. John's Wort extract (standardized to 0.3% hypericin)." (Brown and Foster, "Phytotherapy, Herbal Medicine Meets Clinical Science, Part II," Bastyr University Continuing Professional Education Program, p. 27.)

There are other applications for St. John's Wort. These include: Sciatica, "Pulmonary complaints, bladder troubles, in suppression of urine (for bed wetting), dysentery, worms, diarrhoea, hysteria, and nervous depression, haemoptysis and other haemorrhages and jaundice...Externally for fomentations to dispel hard tumours, caked breasts, ecchymosis, etc." (M. Grieve, A Modern Herbal, Dover Publications, New York, N.Y., 1971, p. 708.) One of the active constituents of St. John's Wort, hypericin, may create photosensitivity in some individuals who generally tend to be fair of skin, however this has not been proven.

St. John's Wort is easily found growing throughout the United

States. There is a theory that the herbs that you find closest to your own door are those that are most beneficial to you. The part most used is the young flowering tops of the plant. Leaves are not as potent as the flowers. Its uses are mystical in nature, and when the yellow flowers are steeped in oil, they mysteriously produce a bright, nearly fluorescent red oil, like blood. While contemporary phytochemists and allopathic scientists are busy attempting to isolate and extract the physical chemical properties of St. John's Wort into the lowest common denominator, its "active constituents" of hypericin and psuedohypericin, there is one element that they cannot duplicate. That is the spirit of the plant itself. As a mystical force in nature, all plants contain a spirit, just as humans do. While the elements of a human body may be isolated in a laboratory, there is missing the "Ki," the spirit, or soul, that is the Divine Essence inherent in the spiritual creation of life itself. The mystery and myth of St. John's Wort are a part of the spiritual, healing nature of the plant, and its gift to humanity in its darkest hours.

"We come out of the Earth, and there's something in the Earth to cure everything. Everything I know I learned by listening and watching. Doctors study what man has learned. I pray to understand what man has forgotten...people seek knowledge instead of wisdom." Vernon Cooper, "The Wisdom Keepers", audiotape edition.

ST. JOHN'S WORT

The Plant of St. Michael: Angelica Archangelica
COMMON NAME
ANGELICA OR ANGELICA OFFICINALIS

"Our knowledge of DNA (deoxyribonucleic acid) explains a lot about herbs and how and why they function. DNA is made up of two microscopic strands which form a loose spiral, the double helix. Stretched out, these strands would be a yard long, but in nature they generally form a spiral within a spiral within a spiral, etc. They are so very compact that forty-six of them will fit into the nucleus of a human cell! When stretched out, this spiral would appear like a railroad track; two parallel tracks held together and apart by 40,000 railroad ties. Each of these ties is made up of nucleotides which carry data. The human cell, when it is first fertilized, contains enough information to reproduce an entire human body.

A plant that for instance is effective in healing the heart, has within its cellular structure the DNA data to reestablish the genetic structure of the heart and reeducate the heart to its proper function.

For each of the forty-four major body organs there are herbs which have the necessary data to renew a human's body season by season. Herbs contain not just vitamins or minerals but are the architects of the organs and contain the blueprints needed to restore the lost information that the body requires to reconstruct the damage brought on by accidents, poor diet, poor inheritance, or old age." Paul Twitchell, Herbs, The Magic Healers, Illuminated Way Publishing, Golden Valley, MN, 1971, p. 27.

Angelica is an ancient plant whose mysterious past is closely connected to many religious traditions. Its earliest ties are believed to be to Syria, then later to its own namesake Pagan Festival, and later to Christianity with the spring-time festival of the Annunciation. According to one legend, Angelica was revealed to humanity by an angel as the cure for the plague. Later it was used in the treatment of typhoid. It blooms on the old-custom feast day of Michael the Archangel, May 8. It was held in such high regard for its healing properties that it was labeled, "The root of the Holy Ghost."

For several years we had this towering, musky smelling mystery plant in our herb garden. Whenever I passed by, I could sense its powerful presence and almost hear its magical voice deep within my senses. It was not until two years ago that we discovered that this magnificent plant was the biannual herb Angelica. It is considered by some herbalists to be one of the most important of the medicinal plants for the treatment of: colds, coughs, pleurisy, wind, colic, rheumatism, anemia, and diseases of the urinary organs. It is a powerful tonic to combat infections and cleanse the blood. An infusion made with the root is utilized for chronic bronchitis, indigestion, and for enhancing the onset of menstruation. (As a uterine stimulant, it should be avoided during pregnancy.) The leaves of the plant when crushed can be applied as a poultice in chest and lung diseases. The stems and leaves, when infused, are useful for a strengthening tonic and aromatic stimulant. The cream made from Angelica is applied to skin irritations. The dried yellow juice of the stem and root is considered valuable in the treatment of chronic rheumatism and gout. It is also reputed to be an agent in the rejection of alcoholic beverages, however, Angelica is used in the preparation of Vermouth, Benedictine, and Chartreuse. In some countries, the leaves are eaten as a bitter spinach, the stalks eaten raw or baked, Norwegians make bread of the roots. It has also an ancient use as a yellow dye. Its cousin, Angelica Sinensis, provides from its roots, the great Chinese tonic herb, dang gui. Because of its natural sweetness, it should be avoided by those with diabetes.

So, how can you use Angelica? If it was so useful for the hopelessness of the plague, perhaps medical science should attempt to test its healing effects upon auto immune diseases such as cancer and AIDS. These are uses of Angelica according to Penelope Ody: "a tincture of up to 3 ml three times a day may assist with bronchitis or flatulence." Dried leaves of the plant infused in hot water as a tea are the "standard dose for indigestion." "Soak a pad in the hot diluted tincture or decoction and apply to painful rheumatic or arthritic joints." (A decoction is made by steeping one to four ounces of the woody parts of the herb in twenty ounces of water boiled and then allowed to simmer for five to twenty minutes. Cool and strain.) Other uses of the decoction are for "anemia, menstrual irregularities or pains, liver stagnation, or weakness." (Penelope Ody, The Complete Medicinal Herbal, Dorling Kindersley, New York, 1993, p.36)

I have used the musky-sweet scented essential oil from the plant Angelica for many applications. One should not use it before going outside in the summer as it attracts insects. I was taught that it is a powerful anti-tumor agent when applied to the reflex points on the feet (where the tumor resides according to Reflexology) or directly applied to the tumor site itself. It is also useful when ten drops are diluted with 25 ml. almond oil for arthritis. Added to the bath, it stimulates circulation and removes toxins. Jeanne Rose relates her uses for Angelica Oil:

"The oil can also be used if you have a stomach ache--either bathe in the scented waters or use one drop...one of my favorite travel and jet lag remedies is a mixture of essential oils that contains Melissa, Angelica, Peppermint, and Ginger. These oils can be mixed together in equal quantities, diluted by half with alcohol, carried on your trips in a small container and when necessary taken. You can also put a drop or two on a compress for headache or stomach ache. This essential oil would be very good used in the diffusor just before a dinner party to stimulate appetite." Jeanne Rose, The Aromatherapy Book, Applications and Inhalations, North Atlantic Books, Berkeley, CA, 1992, p. 67-68)

Angelica is an extremely protective herb, and was considered in its historical context to drive away evil spirits. It has proven its worth as a healing herb throughout its long history. If you have a garden and a bit of room, why not plant an Archangel this spring? The world can certainly use more angels!

HERBAL SPIRIT MEDICINE: TISANE
THE SACRED CEREMONY OF BIRTH RITE TEA

The tea pot is symbolic of the womb. It is round and full, and allows for the creation of nurturing and warmth. Birth Rite Tea allows one to heal the circumstances of conception and birth, like a sacred ceremony of Rebirthing. It allows one to reflect upon the reason the soul accepted this particular assignment into materiality. It links one to their soul's purpose. Meditate and determine the herbs that best represent you or various stages of your soul's growth. Drink this tea with friends or relatives to celebrate your birth. Examples are below:

CEREMONY OF BIRTHRITE

We begin with the gentle essence of the Rose...for its opening is like that of the womb, initially concealing its innermost secret, but when the time is right, gives birth to a powerful medicine...the rose hip. The petals of the gentle Rose are said to nurture the soul.

Chamomile is said to be one of nine sacred herbs given to the world by the god Woden. It prevents weariness of the soul on its journey through life. Chamomile supports, sustains, and encourages life. Its 18 white petals, its rays, surround the yellow of a golden sun, symbolizing hope. For hope springs eternal in the flower of Chamomile.

The essence of Sage insures long life, for it is written in the ancient texts, "Against the power of death, Sage does grow." Sage also allows for wisdom and memory. Its own name defines the individual who, through long life has come to wisdom, the Sage.

The spirit of Yarrow is for protection. It strengthens and purifies the blood. Like our protective layer of skin, Yarrow was also used by the Native American Tribes as a tonic for the skin.

The Yellow Yarrow Spirit allows the knowledge that one is never alone and always protected.

Peppermint is a soothing, cooling herb. It brings forth the balm to comfort and ease the stress and tensions of everyday life. It is a kind friend at the end of a hectic day. The spirit of Peppermint shares its flavor so that we may savor life and refresh our vitality. It represents a sense of balance.

Lemon Balm "comforts the heart and drives away sadness." It lifts spirits and is a great gift to banish melancholy. Its true name is "Melissa," and comes from that same Greek word meaning honey bee. Melissa brings the gift of joy and the hint of laughter.

The brightest of our flower blossoms is Calendula, or Pot Marigold. Its function at this moment is to allow us to see life as an eternal circle. Each petal is a part of that circle, each circle is whole, complete, and ends where it begins. Chief Seattle said that we were all but a strand in the web of life. Each of the petals of this plant symbolizes the circle of ancestors and friends whose courage, love, honor, and support is a celebration our life's creation. Our circle is now complete. We add the flowing mystery of water to the spirit of the plant. As we drink of its essence, we are allowing all of the gifts of each plant to become a part of our own sacred spirit.

HERBAL SPIRIT MEDICINE
HEALING THE SEVEN SACRED BODIES

Create a healing tea formula from the following herbs to heal the Seven Sacred Bodies. I suggest that you share a ceremony with a friend or with loved ones in a sacred circle. It would be most effective to hold such a ceremony on a new moon, as you "plant seeds" to manifest wellness and prosperity. The ancient saying is: the seeds that you plant at the new moon come to harvest at the full moon.

ANGELICA: INTERDIMENSIONAL BODY. Angelica Archangelica is called "The Plant of St. Michael. We invoke its spiritual blessing to assist the Interdimensional Body. Mysterious and towering, legend has it that Angelica was presented to humanity by an angel to cure the plague. Its invocation is: "I invoke the spirit of Angelica to advance my Spiritual Body beyond the limitations of Third Dimensional Reality. All Seven of my Bodies are harmonized."

SAGE: LIGHT BODY. "Contra Vim mortis, Crescit salvia in hortis." This saying from the Middle Ages translates to,"Against the power of death, Sage grows in the garden." Sage, is used as smudge against negativity in certain sacred ceremonies by the Native People. While the White or Green Sage are used in cooking and teas, "Sage the Savior" assists in dis-eases of the liver and blood and enhances memory. The invocation of sage is, "I invoke the immortal power of the sage to move spiritually into oneness with All That Is."

MUGWORT: COSMIC BODY. "Cingulum Sancti Johannis" is believed to be the wrap that John the Baptist wore in the midst of the wilderness. The leaves are burned as Moxas by the Japanese. Burning Mugwort raises the vibrational field for healing. It is a plant (whose leaves were) employed often by the Native People to heal colds, colic, bronchitis, rheumatism, inflammation, wounds, and fever. Invocation: "I invoke the spirit of

Mugwort to integrate my Crown Center with my Soul Star Center. I move beyond the limitations of the ego."

HAWTHORN: SPIRITUAL BODY. Sacred Hawthorn, known as thorn apple tree, earned its sacred status as the crown of thorns that Jesus wore. It is connected in this respect to the Crown Center and its function is reported to heal the DNA of the heart. The invocation of Hawthorn is, "I heal my heart through my Spiritual Body." Hawthorn is for heart.

CHAMOMILE: EMOTIONAL BODY. The Egyptians held Chamomile in High regard, and dedicated it to their gods. Its aroma and tea soothes the Emotional Body through the spirit. It also soothes other plants in the garden where it grows. It is employed for nervousness and hysteria, and is considered sedative. Chamomile contains potassium for the Physical Body as well. The invocation of Chamomile is: "I am peaceful, calm, and tranquil; my emotions are balanced."

ST. JOHN'S WORT: MENTAL BODY. Hypericum, or St. John's Wort is invoked to balance the Mental Body processes and integrate its with all other bodies. Its ancient reputation for casting out "evil spirits" or negative thoughts makes it a powerful agent in preventing depression. Invocation: "My mind is clear, powerful, and integrated as I invoke St. John's Wort."

ECHINACEA: PHYSICAL BODY. Echinacea (Purple Coneflower) is most famous for its use as an immune system stimulant. It assists the Physical Body in its resistance to infections, cancer, diphtheria, and impurities of the blood. It is considered an antiseptic. The invocation for Echinacea is, "I invoke the Spirit of Echinacea to awaken the Change of Consciousness needed for my Physical Body to heal."

MEDITATION ON TWO HANDS

Find yourself with eyes open in peace and silence. Notice your two hands. How many times a day do you see your hands serving you? Be aware of all that they do...they bring the world to you: they answer the telephone, write letters, work, pay bills, they nurture and feed you, clothe you, they drive, pray, and heal. Your hands also reach out to nurture others. In Reiki we are taught to protect and honor our hands for they provide the gateway for the healing touch, the energy that we share. The hands also reflect our evolution and the memories of our ancestors.

Reflect upon the palm of your left hand. This hand holds all of the energy and memory of your mother. See your mother in your left hand, her life, her gift to you of this body, this hand. Show (and feel if you are able) gratitude to your mother for the gift of this body. (pause) See your mother's parents, your grandmother and your grandfather. Show gratitude to them for your life. (pause) Then allow yourself to see their parents, your great-grandparents, as best you can. Show gratitude to them for your life. (pause) Allow yourself to go back through all generations of your mother's family, and give gratitude to all of your mother's ancestors, seen and unseen. Place your left hand upon your heart to share love with all of them throughout all of time.

Reflect now upon the palm of your right hand. This hand holds all of the energy and memory of your father. See your father in your right hand, his life, his gift to you of this body, this hand. Show gratitude to your father for the gift of this body, this hand that serves you. (pause) See your father's parents, your grandmother and grandfather. Show gratitude to them for the gift of your life. (pause) Then allow yourself to see their parents, your great-grandmother, your great-grandfather, and show gratitude to them for your life. (pause) Allow yourself to go back through all generations of your father's family and show gratitude to all of them throughout time. (pause) Then place your right hand also upon your heart.

Say whatever is in your heart that you need to share with

the life streams of your ancestors. Then allow yourself to share your healing Reiki energy with all of your ancestors. (pause)

Place your hands palm to palm. You may say aloud: "We give gratitude to all ancestors who are responsible for the creation of these hands. As I use these hands in service, I honor those who are responsible for the gift of life. (Including the Creator.) As above, so below, may all healing continue..."

VARIATIONS OF THE TWO HANDS MEDITATION

If you are Reiki Level Two or above, you may wish to utilize Reiki symbols for the Two Hands Meditation. You could, for example use the symbol that transcends all space and time, or the symbol that connects us to Universal Consciousness.

HONORING THE MASTERS

On your own, you may choose to show gratitude (by focusing upon both hands) to honor your Reiki Master for the gift of Reiki. Then continue back through their Master, their Master's Master, back to Master Takata, Master Hayashi, Master Usui Sensai, the Tibetan Masters, and the Ancient Ones who taught them.

RIVER OF LIFE

You may choose to focus upon the "lifeline" in each palm for this meditation. In each hand, the lifeline begins near the wrist for our purposes, and curves upward around the thumb toward the index finger. The lifeline could be called the "River of Life" in this meditation.

SACRED MANDALA MEDITATION

"Mandala" in Sanskrit means sacred circle.

It is best if you have a black (the unmanifest void) piece of paper and chalk or a white crayon (White represents energy and light). Draw a circle as large as you can on the piece of paper. The center of the circle is called "bindu" in Sanskrit, which means the beginning and end of creation. Trace your hand(s) somewhere inside the circle. (You may also choose to use parts of the hand rather than the whole hand.) Trace slowly, allowing the tracing itself to be a meditation. Focus on any thoughts that may come to you as you trace each part of the hand or each finger. Meridians begin and end at each finger, so they each have much power and their own energy. The fingertips, I feel, also relate to the past and potentially to past lives. There is an ancient Latin saying:

"Deus in manu omnium signa posuit ut noverint singuli opera sua."

Create the remainder of your mandala with colors and patterns (which could represent your ancestors or your family) that you wish to add.

THE HAND OF BUDDHA

"One day, Siddhartha, the buddha-to-be, felt that he was about to have a breakthrough. Meditating under a beautiful pippala tree, he had the sense that some time that night he would realize full enlightenment and become a buddha. Suddenly, Mara appeared. Mara sometimes appears as doubt, sometimes as anger, darkness, jealousy, craving, or despair. When we feel doubtful or skeptical, he is there. When we feel angry, irritated, or lacking in self-confidence, that is Mara. Siddhartha had been visited by Mara many times before, and he knew that the best way to treat him was to be very gentle.

That day Mara came in the form of skepticism. He said, 'Who do you think you are? You think you can attain great enlightenment? Don't you realize how much darkness, despair, and confusion there are in the world? How can you hope to dissipate all of it? Siddhartha smiled, expressing great confidence. Mara continued, 'I know you have practiced, but have you practiced enough? Who will witness that you have practiced long and hard enough? Who will testify that you can gain enlightenment?' Mara demanded that someone confirm

that Siddhartha was going to become a buddha, a fully awakened person. At that moment, Siddhartha touched the Earth
with his right hand, very deeply, with all of his mindfulness,
and said, 'The Earth will testify for me.' Suddenly, the Earth
trembled and appeared as a goddess, offering him flowers,
leaves, fruits, and perfumes. After that, Earth looked directly
at Mara, and Mara just disappeared.

Even after Buddha attained enlightenment, Mara continued to visit him. One time, after he had been teaching for a
year and a half, he returned to his home town. . . Suddenly
Mara appeared and said, 'Lord Buddha, why don't you become a politician? You can apply your wisdom, knowledge,
and skills as a politician.' The Buddha looked directly at Mara
and smiled, 'Mara, my old friend, I know you well,' and Mara
just disappeared." Thich Nhat Hanh, Touching Peace, Parallax Press, p.41

We must be aware, especially in our Reiki practice, that
each of us may be visited by our own personal version of "Mara."
"Mara" prevents us from realizing our own power and confidence in Self and the Universal Life Force. I have had students say to me, "will this really work for me?" It is the same
question that Mara asked of Buddha. Who will testify for you?
(Or what makes you so special?) You may choose to say, as
Buddha did, "the Earth will testify for me," or "the Light will testify for me." Doubt and fear wear many faces. Even those
whom we love and respect can represent Mara to us. It is not
uncommon for a Reiki practitioner to hear, "what makes you
think you can do this?" from someone in our own family. Please
remember, that is most probably their own personal Mara instead of yours. You have already touched the Earth. Perhaps
it is you who must testify for yourself. Reiki is a great gift, and
accepting it and knowing that you are worthy of this gift is sometimes the most difficult part of the practice. We must be secure
in our practice to share the healing power of love. To fear is to
doubt oneself, for where there is room for fear, it has displaced
love. If you were to look at fear and love as the Yin and the
Yang principle, we only can learn of love through fear, and learn

only of fear through love. Each contains the seed of the other in its core essence. When someone wishes to bring doubt and fear to you, say only, as Buddha did, "Mara, my old friend, I know you well. . ."

SACRED FINGERTIP MEDITATION

Create the sacred "Om" mudra by touching the index finger to the thumb on the same hand. The thumb represents the gateway to Divine Energy, the index finger, the ego self. You are joining ego self with the Divine. With three deep breaths, affirm: as you inhale, say to yourself, "I am one with the Universe." As you exhale say, "The Universe and I are one." This mudra is an excellent way to unite with Divine energy with the power of Reiki when you feel the need for peace in your life. You may also choose to breathe in violet color or energy with your breath to raise your vibration.

Place your fingertips near each other and rest your wrists gently upon your thighs. Each fingertip and thumb tip represents the termination or commencement of a yin or yang meridian in your body. The utilization of mudras to "seal" (mudra means sign or seal in Sanskrit) energy in the body can create more vital energy within the Ki cycle. Think of the Reiki energy flowing.

The fingers should be straight but relaxed, and the thumbs first touch, igniting the flame of the Divine will. Affirm: as you inhale, "I am Divine Will," as you exhale, say, "I release karmic patterns." (Breathe three times, violet color.)

Touch the index finger in such a position that you could imagine a sacred lotus blossom or flame tip of a candle as you gaze down through the shape created by your joined index fingers and thumbs. This could also be considered a sacred "vas", or vase of energy created by the connecting of the energy vortices at the touching of the tips of the index fingers and thumbs. At the touching of the index fingers, affirm, "I expand my consciousness," and as you exhale affirm, "I release ego self." (Breathe three times, orange color)

Touch the Heart fingers together, which are between the index and ringer fingers. Affirm, "I am love incarnate," as you breathe in, as you exhale affirm, "My foundation is solid." (Breathe three times, red color)

Touch ring fingers together and affirm, "I am powerful," and as you exhale affirm, " I am strong." (Breathe three times color indigo.)

Touch little fingers together and affirm, "I am living wisdom," and as you exhale, affirm, "I make wise choices." (Breathe three times emerald green color.)

Now that all fingertips are united, bring them to the Solar Plexus level. Rest the little fingers below the navel and the thumbs above the navel. Allow your focus upon the radiating sphere of yellow-golden energy that is contained in the hands. Fill the Solar Plexus with this radiating energy. Be aware of where it radiates in your body. As you inhale affirm, "I am nurturing Ki," and as you exhale affirm, "I am Divine Fire." (Breathe in and out the yellow-gold fire color as you continue to meditate, drawing the Divine Fire into the central channel called the Sushumna.)

You have created a sacred energy "Vas" in your hands. The word means filled with life, or container of vital life force. I feel that it is important to replenish Ki energy through such a meditation or through the practice of Chi Kung or Tai Chi. The central focus of the energy should be channeled toward the middle of three channels in the body (Sushumna). The Pingala is called the channel of the sun and is on the right side of the subtle body. The Ida is the channel of the moon and is on the left side of the subtle body. They run from the right nostril (Pingala nadi) and left nostril (Ida nadi) all the way down to the base of the spine where they join. The Sushumna channel is suspended between the two and runs from the base of the spine to the top of the head. It is considered to be the most important channel; to attain first attain balance by bringing energy to the center channel of Divine Fire, and then that energy must be channeled from the lower centers upward to the higher centers. In Yoga, the purpose of stretching the spine is to clear the pathway for the Sushumna to channel energy up the spine. Generally the life force flows through the Ida and the Pingala channels while the Sushumna remains primarily dormant. Where the three channels intersect, the major axis chakras are created. It is interesting to consider these subtle body axis braids end at the upper nostril level, the Third Eye Chakra. The Crown Chakra is the culmination of the energy flowing upward. It has no axis braid of its own, and is not considered to exist in some cultural distinctions.

The colors used in this meditation are related to the ancient Yogic texts that refer to each finger as it is related to particular chakras. The basis of the text is as follows:

THUMB: SYMBOL OF GOD OR THE DIVINE, CROWN CENTER

INDEX FINGER: JUPITER, SACRAL CENTER

MIDDLE: SATURN, ROOT CENTER

RING: SUN-MOON, AJNA OR THIRD EYE CENTER

LITTLE: MERCURY, HEART CENTER

LIFE CONTINUES

"Mother I feel you under my feet, Mother I feel your heart beat" From "Fire Prayer" by Denean.

If we are not aware of our connection to Mother Earth, we do not realize that as the trees breathe out, we breathe in. We do not hear the echo of our own breath, our own awareness of our Divine Inter-connectedness with all that is around us. For this moment as you are reading, take a deep breath and realize the importance of your breath, your Prana. There is an ancient Hindu story of the fight of the senses: SIGHT, SMELL, HEARING, TASTE, TOUCH. Cover your eyes for a moment and imagine your life without sight. (PAUSE...) Breathe through your mouth, void of smell, and imagine what your life would be like. (PAUSE...) Cover your ears and imagine no sound whatsoever. Not even the sound of your favorite melody haunts your ears. (PAUSE...) Imagine eating your favorite food without the ability to taste it. (They say that as we grow older, we lose more and more of our sense of taste.) (PAUSE...) Imagine how it would be not to be able to touch and feel the world of texture around you, or even the face of the one you love.

But to continue the story, the five senses were arguing over which of the senses was most important to the quality of life and the body itself. The eyes left, and although the body lost its gift of sight, the body still continued to function. Then the sense of smell abandoned the body, and though the body could not smell, life continued. The ears left the body, and although the body could no longer hear, life continued. Touch and taste left the body in fit of temper, and yet life continued. Then Prana, the breath, offended by the arrogance of those five senses, abandoned the body to teach them all a lesson. Within minutes, the body began to die. All of the senses in a panic, rallied to bring Prana back, and vowed to its utmost importance to the life of the body. Life continues in the breath. You have heard that the breath that you breathe also contains the same molecules of the breath of Christ, the breath of Buddha, and even the breath of Hitler. (The Yin and Yang, the Light and the Dark are represented in the breath as well.) This breath of life is called Prana and as it enters the body's life stream, it manifests life activities in what we call "Ki." But what makes our very breath possible? Is there yet another energy beyond the breath that it depends upon?

How like each of the five senses we humans are. We feel that without us, life could not continue. But if we look deeper, we quickly learn the truth of our expendability. Stand before the oak, the pine, the willow. Lie on the grass and smell deeply of the flowers and the clover. Sense, and smell the freshness of the dew and the spring rain. Feel the warmth of the illuminating sun radiating through the cells of your skin and clothing. Remember even your hair as it is heated by the summer sun. The trees and plants, the sun, the rain, the wind, the birds, the animals, the insects; all part of the Divine plan to sustain the breath of life in a fragile environment.

As the trees breathe out, we breathe in. But without the rich soil, the compost of many forms of life, there could be no life. Without the sun's Light there could be no plant life. Without the wind and the rain there could be no life in the air and in the water. The bird would not sing, the dolphin would not swim, the trees and the plants would not grow. Prana is the breath, but it depends upon the river of life that flows and connects all of us. Are humans arrogant like the senses of smell, taste, touch, hearing, or sight arguing over our most important place in the chain of life? I believe so, for our contribution to the web of life seems to be more of a deficit than a contribution at present.

Be as a willow in the cool morning breeze. Feel your presence in the world around you as solid yet flexible. Know how you shelter birds, insects, and provide shade for the life around you. Sense the fox whose den burrows into the earth in the soil by your roots. Its children grow in the security and warmth of your nurturing presence. Know your neighbors, the stones who slumber in the cool dirt, creating the solid backbone of mother Earth. Feel the underground river flowing deep below the ground, the life blood of the ages. As a Willow, we know our Divine Purpose. Have we humans forgotten our legacy, our reason for being? Have we escaped the web of life only to be condemned to orphan-ship in the world around us?

We must connect to the breath of life...we must connect or drift forever in our forgetfulness. In remembering our place in the web, we can protect, accept, love, and nurture ourselves and other life forms. We can no longer afford alienation as a lifestyle that promotes our ego and our arrogance. Remember that as the tree breathes out, we breathe in. Thank the tree, hug the tree, become one with the tree. It is our ancestor. It is our future. But most important of all, it is our present moment.

Water the seeds of love in your heart. Honor all of life as sharing one breath. We do not want the winged ones: the birds, butterflies, the insects, to leave us. We do not want the land and aquatic animals to leave us. We do not want the plants and trees to leave us. We cannot breathe our concrete and our buildings. These unfortunately represent our legacy to the Earth, our ego creations. Is this what we can be proud of? Prana is life, a gift of Divine Creation. It represents the integration of energies that reflect all of life. Breathe in; be one with all of life around you, the Earth, the sky, the wind, the birds, and the trees. This is life, this is what we are. Alone we cannot survive. Even if we can beat all disease, cheat death our greatest enemy as we see it, and clone ourselves. Even if we can create a tower of Babel that casts a great shadow across the cool Earth. Breathe in and acknowledge that you reflect the Divine in the communion of your breath. Om Namaha Shivaha means "I honor the Divine Within." It is the breath that contains and continues life. We are all Divine creations, none greater than another in actualizing life. We have just forgotten at times who we are. We are the tree. We are the bird. We are the fox. We are the river. We are the soil. We are the stone. We are the vibrant sun shining and the cool star that twinkles at night. Breathe in and Remember.

Breathe in, I am one with all of life
Exhale, I am the vibrant sun shining.

TONGLEN

The word Tonglen translates to "giving and receiving" in Tibetan. In order for this to become a powerful practice, one must first open their own heart and awaken the energy of compassion. The practice of Tonglen involves taking on all the suffering of the person, place or thing that you are working with and giving them love, healing, and well-being in return. This process can be used for the healing of loved ones, the forgiveness of enemies, the healing of ancestors, the animals of the earth, and the earth herself. But you must first have compassion and awaken this energy in yourself. As you do this process you must have a feeling of confidence that this is working and will remove all suffering and pain. It is not always easy to work with this technique, especially when we feel wronged by the other person. There are stages and levels to this practice.

To begin this process of Tonglen, find yourself in a comfortable, quiet place. Begin to quiet your mind. Ask your Guides, Angels, those from the Highest Light (you may ask Jesus, Buddha, or whomever you believe to be beneficial) to be there with you to help with their Greater Wisdom and Divine Love.

Envision before you the person, place, or event. (I suggest that you always begin with the Self.) Feel all this person's pain and suffering, or the suffering surrounding the event. Open your heart with compassion to the person and imagine all the suffering that surrounds them as a mass of grimy, black smoke.

Breathe in a deep breath, and visualize this black smoke drawing into your heart. Your love transmutes or filters that black grime into Light. You exhale this Light back to the other person. Feel this Light as deep compassion, and know that those Higher Beings are participating in this experience as well. Negative karma, and this dark smoke, is purified in the process.

TONGLEN AND REIKI FOR A DYING PERSON

Our western culture is one of the few in the world that does not prepare a person in any way for their death or the death of others. In this respect, fear may become the dominant, suppressed energy present in the dying process. Fear sits in the room of the dying person as the omnipotent, uninvited guest, making everyone uncomfortable. They do not know what to do or say as fear dominates the conversation. A man with cancer told me that his neighbors and friends started to avoid him when they heard from his wife that he had been given six months to live. He confided, "I think they're all afraid of me for some reason, like I'm contagious or something." Dying is an important time, like putting the bow on the package of a life well lived, no matter how long or how short the years may seem. It is an important time to communicate and share, but it is also a time when you can help a person prepare for the separation of the soul from the body (death) and the time thereafter, depending upon their spiritual beliefs. For some people, it may be the first time in their lives that they have had the desire to reflect upon spirituality. A Reiki Practitioner can gently open, balance, and clear the chakras of the Physical Body, nurture the Mental Body, comfort the Emotional Body, and make them aware of the True Self, the Spiritual Body. In Tibetan Buddhism, there are practices for caring for the dead called "rje' dzin." The state of mind of the dying person is considered critical to insure a good rebirth or liberation from the cycle of birth and death. A person should never die with anger, resentment, or strong desires. The practice of Reiki and Tonglen is a good opportunity to assist in eliminating any negative thoughts towards self or others. It is ideal to teach this practice to the dying individual, but if they are not open to it, you can offer to do Tonglen in their presence, like silent prayer, holding their hands. You may also choose to do Tonglen in Absentia. (p. 164) A Reiki treatment can assist in comforting the physical/ mental so that pain does not create negative thoughts or emotions. The focus of the dying process should be upon love.

REIKI AND TONGLEN

In Tibetan Buddhism, there is a concept called "Meditation upon the corpse." In this ancient meditation, contemplatives were sent into the graveyards where many times corpses were exposed and rotting for want of burial. The contemplative would watch the deterioration of the physical body in order to come to terms with fear of death. Later, through detachment, one could imagine the stages of deterioration of one's own body until even the bones were scattered to the wind. Sometimes the bodies in the graveyard were burned, and the contemplative would experience the grimy smoke as it drifted from the corpse. Such burning was sometimes imagined to be the burning away of negative karmic actions. This is the premise of the experience of the dark, grimy smoke that is imagined on the inhalation in the Tonglen meditation. It is as if you are inhaling the energy of negative karmic actions and transforming them to light. Through this compassionate act, one's own karma could also be transformed. The Bodhisattvacaryavatara (which means "engaging in Bodhisattva's <enlightened being> conduct") states:

> "If one does not attempt to truly exchange
> One's own suffering for the suffering of others,
> One will fail to become a Buddha
> And even in samsara (rebirths) will be bereft of happiness."
> (From <u>Bodhicitta, Cultivating the Compassionate Mind of Enlightenment,</u> by Ven. Lobsang Gyatso, p. 69)

Bodhicitta, according to Lobsang Gyatso, is the "compassionate mind which aspires to attain full enlightenment in order to benefit beings." Thich Nhat Hanh calls this watering or nurturing the seeds of compassion in our own hearts. This seed of compassion deep within the heart has also been called "Rigpa."

In Reiki, I believe that we use our Bodhicitta, our compassion, in our very act of channeling Reiki Energy, whether directly in the touch, or in Absentia Healing. In the Absentia Healing process, we also utilize aspects of Tonglen practice. We visualize the suffering individual before us, and channel unconditional love and healing energy to that person. In doing so, through selfless service, negative karma is muted or transmuted, although this is not the motivation. The motivation is compassionate service. The reward of Absentia Healing is often in self-less service.

I will share with you a couple of meditations that I share with students that involve the processes of Tonglen, of "giving and receiving." Please participate in or share these meditations only with those who are comfortable with the process. Taking other people's dark smoke into your own heart as a filter is not a process to commence without prior explanation and meditation. If it serves the Highest Good, and if you or others are willing, Tonglen and Reiki create a powerful energy for transmutation and transformation.

WHAT IS TONGLEN?

The ancient Tibetan practice of giving and receiving is done to relieve suffering. The suffering and healing is both a gift to the object and the subject involved. According to Pema Chodron, there are four distinct stages in the practice:

1. "Flashing openness; a 'natural flash of silence and space. It's a very simple thing.'"

2. "Working with Texture, breathing in dark, heavy, and hot and breathing out white, light, and cool."

3. "Working with relieving a specific, heartfelt instance of suffering."

4. "Extending that wish to help everyone."

In her practice, you are able to get in touch with real, rather than theoretical suffering, and transfer that personal sense of suffering to relieve the suffering of other beings. In doing so, you create more space to come in:

"You breathe out sympathy, relaxation, and spaciousness. Instead of just a small, dark situation, you allow a lot of space for those feelings. Breathing out is like ventilating the whole thing, airing it out. Breathing in is like opening up your arms and just letting go. It's fresh air. Then you breathe the rage in again--the black, heavy hotness of it. Then you breathe out, ventilating the whole thing, allowing a lot of space. What you are actually doing is cultivating kindness toward yourself. It is very simple in that way. You don't think about it, you don't philosophize; you simply breathe in...Without pretending, you can acknowledge that about two billion other sentient beings are feeling the exact same rage that you are at that moment. They are experiencing it exactly the same way that you are experiencing it. They may have a different object, but the object isn't the point. The point is the rage itself. You breathe it in for them so they no longer have to have it. It doesn't make your own rage any greater, it is just rage, just fixation on rage, which causes so much suffering."

"The main thing is to get in touch with fixation. This make's other people's situations accessible and real to you. Then, when it becomes real and vivid, always remember to extend it out. Let your own experience be a stepping stone for working with the world." (Pema Chodron on the Basic Practice, Internet from her book, Start Where You Are, p. 40)

In Reiki, we might try in our practice to extend our experiences outward, and allow each healing we do to flow to all others suffering with similar challenges.

TONGLEN AND REIKI HEALING MEDITATION

Take a deep breath and close your eyes. Imagine yourself in a most sacred place. I imagine myself in an ancient cave in the Himalayan Mountains. One that for thousands of years has been used for sacred, mystical ritual. Smell the scent of incense, sandalwood, and candles burning around you. Feel the powerful presence of ancient Tibetan and Reiki Healing Masters, Enlightened Beings, Bodhisattvas including Kuan Yin (the Oriental Goddess of Compassion) there with you. Feel the compassionate flame at the center of your heart fanning into a warm Reiki fire or torch. See this as a warm sun or fire radiating Reiki Light and Love outward. You may even sense this as white, blue, purple, or gold energy. Say to yourself, "I leave everything in Divine Order, for the Highest Good for all involved in this process. I ask for Divine Assistance."

Now, imagine that you see yourself just as you are standing in front of you. Sense and feel any darkness of the energy of pain, fear, distress, guilt, or suffering as dark, grimy smoke that clouds your essence, your aura. In Sanskrit, there is no word for or concept of guilt. Wrong doing eventually teaches us what is right. Breathe that dark smoke into the fire of your heart, and as you breathe out, exhale Reiki Light and Love energy to that Self that is you. Breathe in the darkness, exhale Light, until all dark energy has been transmuted into Light through the fire and filter of your heart. Feel your Self as both purifying and purified. Allow yourself to proceed with comfortable breath, knowing that you cannot be overwhelmed by this process, only enhanced. To do your best is all that matters, and it becomes easier and easier with each breath.

When you feel clear, imagine another being (plant, animal, mineral, or human) standing in front of you. Repeat the process. See, sense, or feel the texture and darkness of the smoke of pain or suffering that prevents them from healing or actualizing their soul's purpose. Breathe in that dark, grimy smoke right into the Reiki fire or sun at the center of your heart. Continue to breathe in the darkness of this energy and exhale Reiki

Light until only Light remains. Again, proceed at your own comfortable pace, knowing that the process will complete itself when it should. You may decide to work a little at a time with several individuals. Extend this healing outward to all others with similar situations.

Now imagine a situation or event. It can be one that is occurring now, or one that has already occurred in history. Feel and sense that Divine Guidance will allow all involved in this situation or event, as well as the event itself, to be included in the Giving and Receiving Healing process. See the darkness and texture of the grimy smoke of suffering or pain energy that surrounds this event or situation. Breathe in the darkness into the Reiki Torch in your heart, and breathe out Reiki Light. Continue to do so until only Light remains or until you feel that your part of the In-Light process is enough. Extend this outward to all other similar situations.

Sense now that you have the expanded capacity to breathe in the darkness of suffering of all beings (or even Mother Earth and all her beings) into the Reiki flame in your heart. You might consider a culture or group of people instead of all beings. You could even choose your own ancestors as a focus. Sense the grimy smoke of suffering that surrounds these beings. Breathe the darkness into the core of the flame of your heart and as you exhale, exhale Reiki Light. Feel your own negative karma, active, potential, or dormant, evaporating in the process of Giving and Receiving. When the transformation process is complete, thank all who assisted. Feel that it is time to leave the sacred place and return to your own time and place. Breathe the purifying light of the sun into your being three times. Focus on your breath, your body, the warmth in your heart and hands, and return to this moment.

ABSENTIA TONGLEN WITH REIKI ENERGY

Reflect for a few moments about the flame in the center of your heart. Your breath fans that flame into greater illumination. Visualize that you are in a most sacred healing place, and invite or invoke the presence of all your guides, bodhisattvas, enlightened beings, and healing Masters to be there with you. Leave all that you do in Divine Order for the Highest Good.

Center yourself. The following Tonglen of Self Essence is optional: Allow yourself to see that you are standing before your Self. Draw the symbols that you generally use in your Absentia Healing practice. You may draw them with your hand(s), your Third Eye, or on the Great White, Sacred Wall in the sanctuary of your mind. Hold this Self Image between your hands, as if the Self is in a cylinder of Light. Visualize any suffering, pain, sadness, or guilt that clouds your auric field with dark, grimy smoke. The smoke fills the cylinder. Breathe in the darkness that surrounds the Self and fills the cylinder into the flame of your heart and breathe out Light to yourself. Feel your energy field grow more and more clear, until all smoke is gone and the cylinder is clear and filled with Light from your out breath. Your Heart Center has now expanded with Bodhicitta, and is a clearer vessel for transmitting energy as a Reiki channel. You may conclude in your usual manner, or, as I say, "As Above, so Below, may the Healing continue." I release the visual image, and close my energy field by placing my hands palm to palm.

Tonglen of Other: After you are centered and clear, draw the symbols that you generally use in your Absentia Healing practice with your hand(s), your Third Eye, or on the Great White Wall in the sanctuary of your mind. Allow yourself to know that that which serves Divine Order will be served, all sense of ego dissolves into the Light of Service. See, sense, or feel the presence of the person, place, idea, animal, plant, mineral, or event that you wish to focus upon held in your hands there before you in a cylinder of Light. Visualize any darkness of the energy of suffering, pain, sadness, or guilt that clouds the cylinder and the energy field around the person, place, event, animal, plant, mineral, or idea. Breathe in the darkness to the fire in your heart, and breathe out Light. Feel the cylinder grow more and more clear as the darkness is replaced by the Light of your out breath. Your heart expands with compassion, Bodhicitta. You may conclude in your usual manner.

Please note: This Tonglen practice works best if you are focusing upon only one person, place, idea, animal, plant, mineral, or event at a time. However, it is possible to work on related events, a family, an area as a place, such as Mother Earth, or to raise the consciousness of humanity or a particular culture or government. Know that only that which serves the Highest Good will be allowed.

TONGLEN AND REIKI
FOR PAST LIVES AND NEGATIVE KARMA

We can transmute or minimize the effects of negative karma and negative past life experiences by the use of the power of Grace, will, and determination. I believe that self-less service helps to dissolve potential negative karma. In fact, ancient scriptures allude to three different types of karma: potential, active, and dormant. In his book From Death to Birth, Understanding Karma and Reincarnation, Pandit Rajmani Tigunait, states:

"The map laid out in the scriptures tells us that there are three distinct karmic streams: 'sanchita' (dormant) karmas, 'prarabdha' (active) karmas, and 'kriyamana' (potential) karmas. We have the freedom to choose whether or not to entangle ourselves in dormant and potential karmas, but in the case of the active karmas we have almost no choice. That is why it is known as destiny--prarabdha karma is almost impossible to alter. Even those who operate at the level of divine providence and have the power to go beyond the law of karma must not interfere with destiny." (p. 20)

"Yoga texts use another metaphor drawn from archery, to explain the three types of karmas. Sanchita (dormant) karmas are like the arrows stored in a quiver, ready to be fit into the bow. Prarabdha (active) karmas are like the arrows already in flight. Kriyamana (potential) karmas are like arrows that have not yet been made, although all the components are present. Arrows, like any other weapon, are made for a reason. The same reason that impels us to make or purchase arrows impels us to use them. Once they have been shot, the warrior requires more arrows, so more will be made. ..History tells us that there has never been a weapon manufactured that was not eventually used; similarly, once karmas have been created and stored, they must show their effect somewhere, sometime. With weapons, the safest course is to destroy them before the impulse to use them arises. If this is not possible, the next best option is to entrust them to someone who is wise and balanced. This also applies to dormant karmas--the safest course is to either burn them in the fire of knowledge or surrender them to the Divine."

...Some of us do not even want to know about our karmic deeds because we do not want to be called into account by our own conscience. Yet if we remain oblivious to the unmanifest causes of our present problems, we have no way of either eradicating them or preventing other problems in the future. Not knowing the causes of diseases may help us stay free of worry, but it will not prevent us from contracting a disease if we are exposed to its causes. Similarly, ignorance regarding our dormant karmas may give us the illusion that everything is fine, but this illusion will be shattered when our dormant karmas manifest and become active, taking the form of destiny." (p. 25-26)

We have the power, then to affect dormant and potential karma in our lives. When we share Reiki as a channel of Divine energy, I feel that we are affecting these karmas in a positive manner, especially when we do so in Absentia Reiki or in service to the Universe. But we can also impact our own negative karmas in that same way. We can surrender them to "the Divine," (I have included and invocation for 21 days) or enlighten them in the fire of Tonglen and Reiki (either Absentia Reiki or Reiki Meditation). I have included a Reiki Meditation to use the ancient method of Tonglen to heal negative potential and dormant karma. Again, all is left in Divine Order, for the Highest good.

INVOCATION TO RELEASE NEGATIVE
POTENTIAL AND DORMANT KARMA

> You may wish to utilize this Invocation with Reiki Self Treatment, or Absentia Treatment of Self. It may be more powerful for you when it is combined with the Power and Mental Symbols. Repeat each day for 21-200 days.

Negative karma is a lack of love of self and an inability to forgive and release the self from the reflection of former actions. It is guilt in action. Do you love yourself enough to release yourself from this negative judgment and guilt? When you are truly able to forgive and love yourself, then you can be free of the cycle of birth, death, and rebirth. Begin now by invoking the Divine on your behalf. You must ask for any Universal Action, by doing so, you open the gate for Divine assistance. In the Divine Light and Love of the power of the Divine, I now ask Divine intervention on my behalf through Divine Grace to absolve and dissolve any karma past, present, or future, that ties me to the cycle of birth, death, and rebirth into the physical Earth Plane. I ask that whatever needs to be done on my behalf be complete now, and this I claim in the name and the Light of the Divine, for the Highest Good. I love and forgive myself, and ask forgiveness on my behalf of all whom I may have wronged or hurt in the past, present and future. since my birth into individuality.

I ordain this to be so, and, so with the power of Divine Intervention, it is now so. I ask to be filled with the Pure Light and Pure Mind of Love and Compassion. My Divine Soul Essence is purified, restored, and replenished. I honor all of my soul lessons on the Earth Plane as valuable, but now, all that does not serve my Highest Good, any negative karma, soul-limiting vows and contracts or mental-physical agreements, I ask to be reviewed, revoked, and dissolved. And it is now so. This I ask in Divine Order with Divine Assistance. With this freedom from the impact of negative karma, I am now free to fulfill my soul's purpose and help others to claim their own divinity, peace, and power as it serves the Highest Good. I am choosing to be free of negative karma, and through Divine Intervention on my behalf, it is so.

I claim peace, bliss, and enlightenment as my birthright, and sincerely thank all energies that assisted in this In-Light process. As Above, so Below, may the Healing continue.

Invocation Revised from copyright 1994, Karyn Mitchell

KARMA IN OUR DAILY LIVES

"Our karmic challenge, and one that we must remember that we have chosen on some level, is to not only survive the serpent's mouth, but to find peace there. "   Karyn Mitchell

The word karma means"action" in Sanskrit. It is the universal law of cause and effect. We demonstrate our karma everyday in our lives. It is the raging bull, the porcupine, or the pack rat that we unleash upon the world to carry out the patterns of our destiny. Karma presents itself in our thoughts, our words, our deeds. We become creations or actors limited by our own karmic scripts. There is a story of karmic patterns that goes something like this: you are walking along in life when you, unaware, come upon a deep hole, fall into it, and you die. In the next lifetime, you are walking along, encounter the same hole, fall into it, and perish. In the next life, you come upon the same hole, become aware of it, fall into it anyway, and die. This pattern continues until you not only are aware of the hole, but learn how to avoid it and deliver yourself of the action of falling into it to your subsequent death. You take positive action to change the old pattern.

One of the many gifts that Reiki brings to people is that of raising the consciousness to the level of a new perspective. You rise above the "holes" in your life and learn to avoid them. They are old lessons that you no longer need to bring you what you need to learn. The old you who needed those painful repetitive lessons no longer exists. There are no greater affirmations of this principle than those true stories related by students who attend Reiki classes: "I've smoked for fifteen years. I woke up the next day after the Reiki Master Class, and, not only could I not smoke, I had no desire to smoke a cigarette ever again." "I've smoked for thirty years, and I woke up and that was it! No more." "After doing self-treatment every day for two months, my allergies just vanished." "I do not find fault with people anymore." "I am no longer afraid. All of my old fears, including financial ones, are gone." "I am learning to be kind to myself rather than self-destructive." "My addictions (to shopping, drugs, food, attention, whatever...) are gone." "I finally have peace (joy, happiness) in my life." "Negative people or the things that they say no longer affect me." "I left that job that was destroying me, and I have a new job that really fulfills me. I love it!" "I got divorced from an abusive relationship. Now I am happy and free. I only wish I had done this long ago." The dynamic shift in lifestyle and consciousness is a gift, a side-effect of Reiki. It raises the vibratory level beyond the old patterns of negative karma and lifts you up to more Light. It reveals the best of you, the real you, to you. Quitting the struggle to weave the karmic web leaves you with more energy to redirect your life in a positive, interdimensional, rather than linear manner.

In her book, Immortality and Reincarnation, Alexandra David-Neel explains the movement of the soul from lifetime to lifetime as related to karmic actions:

"The namshes is a spiritual entity attached to the material body but not entirely dependent upon it, which separates from it at the time of death and ceases to be usable by it. This namshes will then emigrate and take up residence in another body, 'like one takes off a worn garment to put on another' (Bhagavad Gita)

The namshes is not free, however, to choose the new body of its choice to live in. This decision is imposed on it by the automatic play of cause and effect--the 'game of action' (karma). The causes that determine the nature of its reincarnation are the acts that it has accomplished through the intermediary of the individual with whom it has been united in course of several past lives...

"The shouting of the syllable 'hick!' in a particular tone of voice is said to provoke the namshes to gush out of the crown of the dying person's head, which causes it to be suddenly projected into the Paradise of the Great Beatitude.

"The fashion in which 'hick!' should be pronounced must be learned from a master properly initiated into the secrets of the powa ritual.

"It is said that certain Tibetan yogis employ this procedure to commit suicide. In this way they project their conscious-ness (Namshes) right to the Paradise of the Great Beatitude or another destination of their choice.

Finally, it should also be noted that the Hindus, like the Ti-betans, attach a great importance to the exit of the spirit (namshes, jiva, soul) through the crown of the head. Its exit through any other point of the body is regarded as leading to an unpleasant reincarnation. It is probable that the Tibetans have borrowed this idea from India."(p.63)

It is much like the growth and development of a seed into a flower or a tree:

MEDITATION ON PLANTING A SEED

Close your eyes and imagine that you have just planted a seed. (Positive Reiki Energy) You water that seed daily from the fresh water of the River of Your Life. (Your Ki) See, sense, and feel that you are giving that seedling that is growing much constant sunlight and care. (The opportunity for joy and hap-piness.) You shelter that seedling from unnecessary harsh winds and bad storms. (You protect it from negative energy and personal, critical judgment.) You watch and feel as this grows into a beautiful flower or a strong yet flexible tree. What kind of flower or tree is this? How is it like the new you? Hold this image in your mind and allow it to nurture you and supply you with all that you need in your life for spiritual growth.

CHANGING YOUR LIFE
"How many people do you know who are truly happy?"

There are people who are leading terribly unhappy lives, and yet they seem content that that is their lot in life. They are not aware of the power that they have to reshape their destiny. They are not awake. If you have heard of a Zen alarm clock, I would say that that that is what they need in their lives, a quiet bell that sounds once, waits for three minutes, and sounds again, in ever increasing intervals until you are awakened by its pleasant tones. Unfortunately, it is too often the unpleasant tones that wake people up, the ambulance of life and death situations that forces a person to wake up or die. There is always that choice. If you learn to love yourself (yes, sometimes we must learn this just like we must learn mathematics) and celebrate the Divine Love within you, you may escape the ambulance and all of its drama. You can learn to accept unconditional love from yourself and from others. By realizing your own power, you can gently release negativity from your past, present, and future. You can live a flexible life filled with joy, peace, bliss, and happiness, and understand that this is a conscious choice. I have too often heard people complain that it is difficult to lead a spiritual life in corporate America. I also understand the potential difficultly in leading a spiritual life in all other aspects of living including a trip to the bank, the car dealership, the mall, the bookstore, watching television, or just driving down the street. It has always been a challenge to lead a spiritual life in a materialistic world. In Buddhism, there is reference to the Buddha meditating in the mouth of the serpent. It reflects to us the common challenge not only then, but now, as we are all (potential) Buddhas. The mouth of the serpent is a most challenging place to be, let alone to meditate there. Our karmic challenge, and one that we must remember that we have chosen on some level, is to not only survive the serpent's mouth, but to find peace there.

I was especially proud of a Reiki Master named Cathy who dramatically reshaped the direction of her life and her karma following an especially traumatic child and adulthood. She stated that prior to Reiki, her life had been an out-of-control tornado. Chaotic events and negative people were constantly spinning around her creating constant turmoil and strife in her personal life. After Reiki, she reclaimed her power, her destiny, and her soul's purpose. She now says with much humor, "The tornado is still out there. It is just that I am in here, in the center of it all, peaceful, calm, and unaffected by the gale-force winds that blow around me. I guess that you could say that I am the 'eye of the tornado,' just there and watching others spin out of control around me. I choose not to get involved in their negative actions." And therein lies the true awareness. We can only be responsible for our own actions, and choosing not to react to the drama of others is a way to avoid old karmic patterns. If you remove yourself from the dysfunctional chess match, believe me, the game will not end there. It will continue with or without you. Eventually we learn, as the Kenny Rogers song goes, "You've got to know when to hold 'em, know when to fold 'em, know when to walk away, know when to run..." Life is about recognizing karmic actions, karmic patterns and games, and learning to empower and honor the self. If we are too busy playing dysfunctional games with other people, we do not have time to pursue our soul's purpose. Our Soul Train becomes derailed easily by others or negative events in our lives. We cannot expect others to put our train back on the track. Nor can we continue to blame others for events that cause us to suffer. We must learn to shelter our soul from life's storms that rage around us. There is a poem/song written by Thich Nhat Hanh that I find particularly powerful:

WARMTH
I hold my face, in my two hands. (repeat)
My hands, hollow
To catch what might fall from within me,
Deeper than crying.
I am not crying

I hold my face in my two hands (repeat)
To keep my loneliness warm,
To cradle my despair,
Shelter the flame
From the rain and the thunder,
Warming the place
So that tomorrow may blossom compassion.

(This is part of the poem as sung by Sister Chan Khong)

KARMIC BLACK HOLES

In Reiki Level I, I relate my theory of energy loss. It goes something like this: You wake up in the morning, and if you've had a good night's sleep, you have a full container, much like a quart can or container of V-8 Vegetable juice, of energy. You are well-rested, replenished with energy, and ready for your day. During your peaceful morning shower, the phone rings. Still dripping wet, you frantically race to answer it. It is someone trying to sell you something. You are angry for the disruption of your peaceful shower and the intrusion upon your valuable preparation time for work. You have just allowed holes of anger to be punched into your precious container of energy. Your energy is now leaking out because of this anger. On your way to work, you are held up in a traffic jam, and, as you gaze at the minutes ticking by on your clock, you are worried that you are going to be late for work and perhaps even chastised by your company for your tardiness. Your energy is now leaking out because of this worry, which is related to a probable event that may never occur. You arrive at work with perhaps a half of a container of energy to begin your work day. By one o'clock or perhaps even two o'clock, you are exhausted because you lost half of your energy supply of the day by eight o'clock a.m. from the impact of anger and worry energy loss.

Other aggravations such as stress from work also contribute dramatically to the loss of energy. One of the major causes of stress is the desire to be perfect, to go beyond what is realistic for us to achieve. We do not honor or are not sensitive to our physical and mental limitations. We lose our energy by putting too much pressure on the container, to extend beyond our energy capacity, and we get deficit energy. The container, the can gets crushed by sucking out more than it contains. It crushes from the inside out. It implodes. Over time this develops into an overwhelming situation called chronic fatigue syndrome. It takes an immense amount of time and energy to heal such an abused, crushed can.

We can make excuses for all of the energy loss in our lives.

I have a quotation in our healing center that is from Richard Bach's book, Illusions: "Argue for your limitations, and sure enough, they're yours." The events that drain our energy do so because we allow it to happen to us. We have the power to turn the ringer off on the phone during certain hours. We have the ability to say to ourselves, "So what if I am stuck in traffic, there is not a thing that I can do about it. It is a good time to meditate listen to Mozart, read a good book, etc..." We could even consider a red light a gift of reflection and a good time to pause, stretch, and take a deep breath. There is an ancient saying, "Don't push the river, it flows by itself." This means, allow the flow, an Oriental philosophy called, "Wu Wei." I suggest that if you are faced with a stressful situation that you take in a breath and say to yourself the word/syllable "Wu." As you exhale, breathe out the word "Wei." You could even imagine that you are breathing in a particular color that denotes peace, such as the color blue. We must be responsible to protect our energy from the black holes that are a part of our karmic vision. We have created a world of stress and intrusion as a part of our karmic vision. It is a lesson that can teach us about what we allow to happen to us from moment to moment in our daily lives. While we have our own personal karma, we all share a common karmic vision with others in our culture, our workplace, or even in our family. These perceptions of what our lives should be like are a part of this vision. It is real to us, but may be perceived as much different by others who share our reality. One person's Heaven may indeed be another's hell. It is a matter of karmic vision or perception. There is a short poem that goes, "Two men look out of prison bars, one sees mud, the other stars..." This is why it is of utmost importance that we begin to honor our energy as it manifests our destiny through karma. The opposite is also true to an extent. Our karmic destiny is manifested via our energy. In Tibetan Buddhism, there is reference to "hungry ghosts" and the realm of hungry ghosts. These ghosts exist because of greed, wherever people are never satisfied, especially with what they have or what they are. What causes you to give more energy than you have available for money? Are you feeding a hoard of hungry ghosts? What is the purpose? Perhaps if we feel we make enough money, we can buy our way out of death, or at least delay it. Sogyal Rinpoche in his book, <u>The Tibetan Book of Living and Dying</u> states:

> "Why do we live in such terror of death? Because our instinctive desire is to live and to go on living, and death is a savage end to everything we hold familiar. We feel that when it comes we will be plunged into something quite unknown, or become someone totally different. We imagine we will find our selves lost and bewildered, in surroundings that are terrifyingly unfamiliar. We imagine it will be like waking up alone, in a torment of anxiety, in a foreign country, with no knowledge of the land or language, no money, no contacts, no passport, no friends...

> "Perhaps the deepest reason why we are afraid of death is because we do not know who we are. We believe in a personal, unique, and separate identity; but if we dare to examine it, we find that this identity depends entirely on an endless collection of things to prop it up: our name, our 'biography' our partners, family, home, job, friends, credit cards...It is on their fragile and transient support that we rely for our security. So when they are all taken away, will we have any idea who we really are?" (p. 16)

I know of a woman, whom I will call Judy, who was making over $250,000 a year and was always in debt and worried about money. She never had enough money, and it seemed she never really knew where her money was going. Perhaps she had a black hole in her purse. Many people do. Judy was so miserable in her job, yet she still had to continue, she believed, to pay her bills and her debts. Her boss was abusive, and her work load was unbelievable. She worked in energy deficit. One day Judy went to a local grocery store, and met a checkout clerk who was actually happy in her work. (How many people do you know who are truly happy?) The next day, she was compelled to return to that store to find out the secret of that woman's happiness. After all, how dare she be happy, especially clerking in a grocery store where you many times experience people at their worst. Judy made a small purchase and stepped up to her register. The woman again appeared to be happy. Judy asked the woman what made her so happy. The woman did not seem to be surprised by this question, and Judy thought perhaps she had been asked the same question before. The woman told her her story in just a matter of minutes: a battle with cancer, an abusive husband who walked out on her when she was diagnosed with cancer, her problems with her insurance company and her doctor bills, and her bouts of frequent depression because of all of that. Then she told her secret. She said, "I turned everything around in my mind. I tried to look at all of the gifts the bad things had brought to me. For one thing," she laughed, "it took care of the abuse from my husband. I called that the gift of freedom. The cancer made me look at and celebrate the days when I did feel good. The bills led me to bankruptcy. With money, once you have nothing, everything looks good to you. You learn not to depend upon it for happiness. I learned three things, two that I will share with you: 1.) I am not my money, and 2.) I am not my cancer. I had to define my self as me, no more, no less."

In Buddhism, there is one premise that is common to all schools of Buddhism. That is the law of "Impermanence." Suffering comes because we do not understand that everything changes. Even diamonds eventually return to coal. One moment we may be rich and have everything in material terms, but the next moment we may lose it all. The way to overcome suffering is to recognize that things change and not to get too attached to anything. Judy was too attached to her definition of her life in terms of money. She was feeding hungry ghosts that she did not even recognize. The clerk in the grocery store had lost her hungry ghosts and her attachment to money. She was experiencing her life in terms of each moment. Her cancer had brought her to some kind of reconciliation with the notion of her mortality. He loss of relationship and money had taught her how quickly things that don't really matter can change. The clerk works now to meet people who might be suffering as she did, and brighten their day in any way that she can. You might say that her motivation has changed, but it is much more than that. She studied Reiki, and believes that Reiki, and quite specifically self healing, saved her life. (Her doctors say that she experienced a spontaneous remission.) Her perspective of death has now brought her the freedom to live. They say that when a person faces not just the notion but the closeness of their death, they gain a different perception of priorities. For example, if you were facing the closeness, the breath of death with three days to live, would you drive through a traffic jam to get to work to draw a paycheck? I doubt it. That is, unless you truly LOVE your job, as some people do. What would you do with that precious short time? Would you consider those three days a blessing or a curse? I suggest that you give that thought some careful consideration, and even ask a few significant others what they would do with their three days of life.

It is our ego of separation that keeps us from understanding what is truly important in life. It is our ego that keeps us from understanding who we are and what we truly need to be peaceful and happy. According to Sogyal Rinpoche, the Tibetan concept for ego is called "dak dzin," which means "grasping to a self." In <u>The Tibetan Book of The Living And Dying</u> he states:

> "So ego then, is the absence of true knowledge of who we really are, together with its result; a doomed clutching on, at all costs, to a cobbled together and makeshift image of ourselves, an inevitably chameleon charlatan self that keeps changing and has to, to keep alive the fiction of its existence...The fact that we need to grasp at all and go on and on grasping shows that in the depths of our being we know that the self does not inherently exist. From this secret, unnerving knowledge spring all our fundamental insecurities and fear. So long as we haven't unmasked the ego, it continues to hoodwink us, like a sleazy politician endlessly parading bogus promises, or a lawyer constantly inventing ingenious lies and defenses, or a talk show host going on and on talking, keeping up a stream of suave and emptily convincing chatter, which actually says nothing at all. Lifetimes of ignorance have brought

us to identify the whole of our being with ego....Ego plays brilliantly on our fundamental fear of losing control and of the unknown...To end the bizarre tyranny of ego why we go one the spiritual path. The truth is simple, and the teachings are extremely clear... But as soon as we enter what I call the "Kitchen Sink" period of the spiritual path, and the teachings begin to touch us deeply, unavoidably we are faced with the truth of ourselves. As the ego is revealed, its sore spots are touched, and all sorts of problems will start arising. It's as if a mirror we cannot look away from is stuck in front of us. The mirror is totally clear, but there is an ugly, glowering face in it, our own, staring back at us. We begin to rebel because we hate what we see; we may strike out in anger and smash the mirror, but it will only shatter into hundreds of identical ugly faces, all still staring at us." (From : Tibetan Book of Living and Dying by Sogyal Rinpoche, Harper Collins, NY, NY, 1993, p118.)

We must begin to see ourselves and the reality that we have created as an evolutionary process. We can learn to protect our energy and our lives from the negativity that exists around us, We can learn about the black holes of karma, of our own doing and our own direction, and create a new reality based upon what is truth rather than fiction. We must ask ourselves, have I come here to this life for a reason? If I have come here with a purpose, what is that purpose? Life is an evolutionary process. We come to learn of love. The first and most difficult step is to love the Self beyond the ego, unconditionally. And when we do, perhaps the karmic mirror of the soul will reflect love back to us.

"HUMAN beings, born ultimately of the stars and now for a while inhabiting a world called Earth, have begun their long voyage home." CARL SAGAN

MEETING YOUR SIMULTANEOUS AND FUTURE SELF

Recently I discovered in a meditation that a guide who had assisted me many times in the past was none other than the same guide who was finally introduced to me as my "Future Self."

If you experience enough Past-Life Regression Therapy, you eventually understand the spiritual evolutionary process. But another thing may happen. You may become aware that you are a time traveler. I have heard that time is just a way to keep everything from happening all at once. I believe that it happens simultaneously whether we are aware of it or not. It is just our perception that keeps it segregated. You have the ability to heal karmic and traumatic events from your past lives. You can do this by acting as a spiritual guide and healer for your Past-Self. Oftentimes in Regression Therapy, if the experiencer is Reiki, I will ask that this experiencer offer Reiki healing to the Past-self who needs healing. It proves to be extremely powerful. Just as you can transmit Reiki healing into the future (<u>Reiki, A Torch In Daylight</u>, Reiki Level II, p. 79) you can also transmit Reiki to the past to heal yourself, history or past events, or to those whom you perceive as your ancestors. It can be an experience much like waking or lucid dreaming, where you walk into the dream and become an active participant, in this case, a healer. Much like the practice of ancient Shamanism, you can become a multidimensional "walker" in three worlds. Past, present, and future merge in the present moment, where you can participate in the activities of the lower, middle, or upper worlds. You can transcend the space-time continuum, as we who practice Reiki often do in Absentia Healing. (We can utilize the symbol for Universal Consciousness, as well as the symbol that transcends all of space and time.)

The Hawaiian Huna tradition that Serge King speaks of in his book, <u>Mastering Your Hidden Self</u>, consists of many types of dreams and dream states:

"The most common word for 'dream' is 'moe 'uhane,' which

literally means 'spirit sleep.' A code meaning is 'the spirit breaks away and goes elsewhere.' Specifically, it refers to the dreams you have during a deep, sound sleep. According to Hawaiian tradition, your spirit goes traveling, seeing persons and places, encountering other spirits, experiencing adventures, and passing on messages from your 'aumakua' or High Self. All of these events you remember as dreams.

Among the many sorts of dream experiences are messages from the subconscious relating to our state of health and suggesting how to improve it. Other dreams from the same source concern our relations with other people and the state of our beliefs about ourselves and the world we live in. Certain dreams come directly from the High Self, though still interpreted by the subconscious. These tell us about our spiritual progress and sometimes give us foreknowledge of things to come."(p. 123)

A recurrent dream for me in my years of Reiki involve the actual hands-on healing practice or teaching of Reiki. One night in Curacao, Netherlands Antilles, I had the dream that I was in my pajamas performing a Reiki treatment on a client in the states. The shirt of the pajamas had a distinctive figure of a hawk on the front of it. I became aware after about thirty minutes into this "dream" that I was not wearing suitable clothing for a professional Reiki treatment. In some fashion, I called myself back in the middle of the treatment to change into more suitable attire. I do not remember completing the treatment. On my return to the states, the client recounted to me a dream that they had had. They went to bed under much stress with the final thought, "I could really use a Reiki treatment. Too bad Karyn is out of the country." It seems that I walked into their bedroom with my Reiki table already in place, and commenced a Reiki treatment. "Two things were odd," the client remarked. You were wearing a shirt with a big bird on it, and you left in the middle of the treatment. The client said, that is how I knew it was just a dream, because otherwise, it sure seemed like a Reiki treatment, and the next day I felt great. I have ceased attempts to analyze these dream experiences, and now accept them at face value most of the time. I also spend a great deal of time healing animals who have been hurt or wounded. That is why I have a particularly difficult time with the concept of hunting for "sport." I now know beyond a doubt that there is a karmic energy that insures that what we hurt we may become, and it does not matter what that life form may be. If you have knowingly hurt another life form, you may choose to transmit Reiki to your former consciousness as well as the injured animal, plant, mineral, or human.

I found that dreams may also take on an energy of transmigration. Nearly three years ago, I was experiencing a sudden onset of depression for no apparent reason. I had studied the various aspects of depression in college, and was able to recognize the signs. However, I was unable to uncover any reasonable mental, emotional, or physical reason for this downward spiral. Then it occurred to me to consider the fact that my depression may have a spiritual cause. I decided to ask for guidance and understanding. In meditation I could not receive an answer, but two nights later, in a dream, I walked into a room that appeared to be somewhere in an old hospital. I remember distinctly the row of beds in this room, each bed occupied with a suffering person. I walked immediately to a bed on the south wall. I could see the paint peeling off the wall, the twin, steel bed, and the small woman dying there. She looked up at me and smiled weakly, as if she recognized me. At that moment, I recognized her. She was that internal voice that explained my sudden passion in the past year for India, the Hindu religion, and Satha Sai Baba. It was her calling out to me with love, through space, to come to her side to help her die. Somehow we were able to communicate without speaking. I was there, although invisible, to those who attended to her physical needs, but no one else came to visit her. She was very much alone. In whatever way it was possible over the next few weeks, I visited her nightly, sharing Reiki with her and helping her to find comfort and peace. I was with her when she left her body in death. I do not believe that any of us die alone. As her soul left that ancient, tired body, she thanked me with her eyes for my attendance. I saw her "Light" move to a Greater Light that existed beyond the Bridge of Light. After her death, my depression evaporated like a fine mist. I felt that I had never really received a complete answer to my quest for greater understanding of the cause of my depression. So, once again I asked for guidance. This aged, dying woman, it seems, was a simultaneous life existence. It was another me, if you would, suffering and dying alone in India. I know that there may be many ways to dissect this notion psychologically or intellectually, but spiritually, I know that that woman who cried out to me in her darkness was me.

I know this phenomenon exists because I have since met another, younger "me" who lives in Amsterdam. I know that she is me just as certainly as I know that the reflection in the mirror is not someone else. I visited her twice without detection, but the third time she saw me or my energy form. I know that my visit scared her to some extent, as she thought I was a ghost. I have not traveled there since, and feel that avoiding her from then after was somehow a conscious choice on my behalf.

Whether you believe that simultaneous lifetimes are possible is more of a willingness to accept the fact that we are unlimited beings. Fritjof Capra, in <u>The Tao of Physics</u> offers a perspective from the Eastern traditions:

"The most important characteristic of the Eastern world view--one could almost say the essence of it--is the awareness of the unity and mutual interrelation of all things and events, the experience of all phenomena in the world as manifestations of the same ultimate reality. The Eastern traditions constantly refer to this ultimate, invisible reality which manifests itself in all things, and of which all things are parts. It is called Brahman in Hinduism, Dharmakaya in Buddhism, Tao in Taoism. Because it transcends all concepts and categories, Buddhists also call it Tathata, or Suchness:
'What is meant by the soul as suchness, is the oneness of the totality of all things, the great all-including whole.'" (p. 130-131)

I find it fascinating and an honor that these other beings were revealed to me, I feel that I had to meet the second "me" to understand the energy relationship that was possible in the splitting or fragmentation of the soul. I know that the first "me" not only existed, but was another aspect of my own soul. I have invested a great deal of time considering the implications and complications involved in such an encounter with other selves. I have decided not to judge those encounters or experiences. I entertain a gnawing suspicion that all of us and even more of life beyond my comprehension, are yet another "me." Somehow I do know that there are other simultaneous "me's," and I am willing to help them when they most need assistance, trusting that these encounters will be in Divine Order, for the Highest Good. If such an encounter is not for the Highest Good, I trust that it will not happen. We must remember to always ask for what we need to know and trust that it will be revealed to us.

As Kahlil Gibran the poet so eloquently stated, "Trust the dreams, for in them is hidden the gate to eternity." Dreams are held in high regard in many cultures and belief systems. In one particular oriental religion, it is believed that dreams assist one in healing. They do this by chelating out of the system of the individual any negative or potentially harmful energy. In this respect, nightmares are regarded as positive experiences as they cleanse the soul of negative energy that has penetrated the consciousness. One releases darkness during the sleep/dream state. When the individual awakens, they are much lighter physically, mentally, emotionally, and spiritually.

In his book, <u>Far Journeys</u>, Robert A. Monroe describes an out-of-body-experience in much the same way that my active dream encounters occurred:

> "What is the out-of-body experience? For those who have not encountered the subject as yet, an out-of-body experience (OOBE) is a condition where you find yourself outside of your

physical body, fully conscious and able to perceive and act as if you were functioning physically--with several exceptions. You can move through space (and time?) slowly or apparently somewhere beyond the speed of light. You can observe, participate in events, make willful decisions based upon what you perceive and do. You can move through physical matter such as walls, steel plates, concrete, earth, oceans, air, even atomic radiation without effort or effect.

"You can go into an adjoining room without bothering to open the door. You can visit a friend three thousand miles away. You can explore the moon, the solar system, and the galaxy if they interest you. Or--you can enter other reality systems only dimly perceived and theorized by our space/time consciousness. " (p. 3)

Be open to the experiences that lead you beyond what you perceive as reality. As you open the doors of your awareness and perspective of reality, you gain new insight and expand spiritually into the self as unlimited existence and potential. It is most difficult in our mainstream culture to see beyond the inside of the cultural or religious silo, but it is the only way to achieve freedom of thought and spirit.

It is important to remember that fear becomes quite a viable, negative energy or entity whenever we challenge the constraints of that silo. We recently attended a performance at the comedy club, "Second City" in Chicago. One humorous satire involved a creative individual who was "mainstream impaired." He did not watch television, did not care to purchase the products he was supposed to covet, and, in short, was considered a threat not only to himself, but to society in general. What would happen if his ideas caught on and became "mainstream?" The economy would fail and people and their activities could not be so easily programmed. In the end, this radical was given an operation to remove a gram of his brain. His first words were, "I'm going out to buy a Jeep!" The doctor pronounced him cured of his terrible dis-ease of "mainstream impairment." How programmed are we in our culture? Perhaps we who are Reiki might consider transmitting healing energy to release such manipulation. I am convinced that re-evaluating programmed beliefs is just as powerful as healing past life patterns that are electric with karmic repercussions. Blindly accepting what others want us to believe can be just as dangerous as falling into the same hole lifetime after lifetime. In fact, it is one of those holes, and we can become victims of our own holy war. Lifetime after lifetime, we may choose to embrace the cause at hand, whether it be the search for the Holy Grail that inspired the "Holy" War, or joining an organization that proclaims that its beliefs are the only truth. There is a much misunderstood statement in the philosophy of Buddhism that says, "If you find Buddha on the road, kill him." This statement is not to promote violent acts, but rather to dramatize the notion that any "Buddha" outside of the Self would be a false buddha. The concept of Buddha is merely the suggestion that we can become our Highest Form. Buddhists do not keep statues of Buddha about for any other purpose than to reflect back to them or make them mindful of the fact that they can achieve their highest potential. The statue is no more than a reminder or a mirror of one who has already achieved this In-Light-in-ment. No one else can do this for you, it is your path, your road, and you must walk it. There are times when you are presented with a fork in the road. The fork represents questioning or departing from old patterns of life or belief systems. We must choose between the comfortable old road or the challenge of exploring the new Way. It is what Robert Frost addressed in his poem, "The Road Not Taken":

> "I shall be telling this with a sigh
> Somewhere ages and ages hence;
> Two roads diverged in a wood, and I--
> I took the one less traveled by,
> And that has made all the difference."

I was attending a mindfulness retreat called "Pain, Love, and Happiness," with Thich Nhat Hanh in Santa Barbara when I received the news of Mother Teresa's transition. There, sitting with my Dharma Discussion Group on the grass beneath a fragrant Eucalyptus tree on a perfect California day, I cried. I felt such a sense of loss for this dedicated woman whom I had never even met. She had been there for so many who were dying and suffering. For several days of the retreat, I had been living in silence, knowing that out in the "world" many people were also mourning the death of Princess Diana. Especially her two sons, who would now grow beyond their teen years without their mother. It was just that thought that led me to the realization of how we live on, not only in our children, but by the deeds that we do and the way that we live our life. Life continues in the energy of what we have created. Life continues. It is a circle with no beginning and no end. To live purposefully is to die with purpose. To live in consciousness is to die consciously. It was often the practice of Zen Masters to compose their own death poem prior to their transition. One such poem was written in 1360 by Zen Master Kozan Ichikyo:

> Empty-handed I entered
> the world
> Barefoot I leave it.
> My coming, my going--
> Two simple happenings
> That got entangled.

I used to mourn in the late fall for the trees as they lost their leaves, for the grass and the plants kissed and dying by the first hard frost. All that remained of the summer's fragrant beauty, warmth, and bounty was now only a memory that I visited in my sadness. This mourning even after a lifetime of knowing that just as surely as the frost killed, the potential of new life, the sleeping buds and seeds of what had been, would bring new life in the spring. As a part of nature, we also continue in the seeds of what we have planted, what we have created with our compassion.

"Everything is in transformation. We are all children of the Earth, and, at some time, she will take us back to her again. We are continually arising from Mother Earth, being nurtured by her, and then returning to the Earth. Like us, plants are born, live for awhile, and then return to the Earth. When they decompose, they fertilize our gardens. After six months, compost becomes fresh vegetables again. Plants on the earth rely upon each other...It also depends on us. Our way of walking on the Earth has a great influence on animals and plants. The future of all life, including our own, depends on our mindful steps." Thich Nhat Hanh, "Environment is Interbeing," "Mindfulness Bell" #7, 1992

MEDITATION ON THE PATH

Close your eyes and be at peace with yourself and the world. Allow yourself to view your past experiences and perhaps even your past lives as a traveler, a journeyer. You have with you only a walking stick to steady yourself, and perhaps a bundle or pack with your most prized possessions. The day is sunny and bright, a warm spring morning. You are walking slowly up the familiar Path of Your Life. Be aware of the nature of that path. Even if this path is complicated or challenged with rocks or holes, you are still comfortable with it as you know it, the way is familiar to you. It is a part of your history, your destiny.

But now, you become aware of something different. You have thought a new thought, a new idea, or perhaps even looked in a different direction. There is suddenly a boulder that creates a fork in the path ahead that was not there the last time you passed this way. You pause for a moment and sit upon this boulder contemplating your next step. You are aware that there are now two paths available to you where before there was just one. Be aware of the emotions that surface deep inside of you. What would you call these emotions? Are they fear? Doubt? Concern? Agitation? Or does this new perspective offer you a sense of excitement and hope? Look ahead at the path that you already know so well. Does it really represent you as you are now? Meditate for a moment upon the old path. It reflects the knowledge, the awareness, the judgments, and the belief systems that have been presented to you by others. Are you still comfortable with those beliefs, or are you ready to challenge yourself with the new path? Should you reevaluate old patterns of thoughts and old beliefs and only travel the new path? Should you be able to walk in between both paths, creating a new path which embraces a sort of middle way? Ask a Guide, a Master, or even your Future Self for guidance or perspective. Review old thoughts and belief systems. Do they prevent you from obtaining your Highest Good or greatest potential in any way? If so, challenge these old systems with the energy of Light and Wisdom. Put Reiki into the situation, and continue to do so until the Way is clear for you. All paths lead eventually to the place where we need to be, a place of unconditional Love. Be patient and know that you will arrive Home sooner or later.

If you are content with your process, you may open your eyes when you are ready. Otherwise, you may stay in that place as long as you choose to contemplate your Truth. Be at Peace.

MEDITATION TO MEET YOUR FUTURE SELF

Close your eyes and look inward to the flame burning deep in the center of your heart. Expand that flame with every breath, as you breathe in Peace and breathe out Light. You are filled with Peace and surrounded by the Light. Our intentions are left in Divine Order and for the Highest Good. Our purpose is to meet our own Future Self, and if it is so ordained, we call forth that energy to be with us at the appropriate time, or when we reach the Bridge of Life.

Just ahead of you, you see, sense, or feel a cool, blue pond on a windless day. The sun shimmers across the surface of that pond, reflecting tranquility. You are aware of the sounds of the day that surround you, the birds in the distant trees, the wind as it brushes through the leaves, and the beat of your own heart warm in your chest. You notice a small pebble on the ground before you. You pick it up and hold it gently in the palm of your hand. You drop it quietly into the water and watch as it slowly and silently drifts down through the blue of the water, down to the floor of the pond. You are still and quiet, resting in deep silence.

You lift your gaze and notice a small stream to the north that feeds this pond. You follow a narrow trail until you come to an ancient arched, stone bridge. It seems familiar to you, perhaps from dreams or from a former existence. It is the Bridge of Life. You step upon the thick wooden planks that create the backbone of the bridge, and as you reach its crest, you are aware that someone is approaching you from the other side of the bridge. At first glance it seems that you recognize, that you know this person. They are smiling now as they stand before you. You notice what they are wearing and what they look like. If you choose to ask them their name, and you sense, feel, see, and know this name. You may then ask if they are your Future Self. If it is time for you to meet your Future Incarnation, you have just done so. If not, we ask that when it is the appropriate time that your Future Self be made know to you.

I now ask, in Divine Order, that if you have lost any part of yourself or your energy body through time, or if you have allowed someone to take any part of you, or if any part of you was stolen, that you accept a symbolic gift from your Future Self. This returned energy may look like something that belonged to you from your past, or it may appear as Light or colored energy. I ask that if it serves your highest good, that you accept this energy and place it where it needs to go to allow you to be whole, healed, and happy. You deserve to be whole, healed, and happy. Fill your Physical, Mental, Emotional, Spiritual, and Interdimensional bodies with this energy gift. If there is anything else that you need, for any of those bodies, I ask that this Guide present you with it now. If there is anything that you are ready to be made aware of to heal your karma, I ask that it be revealed to you now. Trust that your Future Self will only reveal positive awareness and great love. Listen deeply with your heart, and know that you are directed onto the right path to learn and heal. You may choose to ask your Future Self to assist you in your spiritual growth; you may ask for the next step in your evolution when you are ready for it. You may even choose to ask your Future Self to clear, harmonize, and align your chakras. Share your love with this Future Self, and feel the comfort in knowing that life is continuous.

As you prepare to return, be aware of and maintain the energy of Higher Consciousness that was shared with you. It is a deep Wisdom from the heart that transcends knowledge of the mind. Embrace your Future Self if you choose to do so, and turn back to your side of the Bridge of Life. Step back across the Bridge of Life, follow the Path of Enlightenment back to the pond that reflects truth and beauty. Pause for a moment and look deeply into this pond. Allow it to reveal your True Self to you. The True Self whose energy and Light greatly resembles that of your Future Self.

Take a deep breath and allow yourself to slowly return to your present time, your present place. You are awake and aware now, with your eyes open, you see things in this place and time as they really are.

HUM

ANIMALS, PLANTS, AND MINERALS

Reverence for Life
" The First Precept, Reverence for Life"

Aware of the suffering caused by the destruction of life, I vow to cultivate compassion and learn ways to protect the lives of people, animals, plants, and minerals. I am determined not to kill, not to let others kill, and not to condone any act of killing in the world, in my thinking, and in my way of life."[31]

"Life is precious. It is everywhere, inside us and all around us; it has so many forms.

The first precept is born from the awareness that lives everywhere are being destroyed. We see the suffering caused by the destruction of life, and we vow to cultivate compassion and use it as a source of energy for the protection of people, animals, plants, and minerals. The First Precept is a precept of compassion--karuna--the ability to remove suffering and transform it. When we see suffering, compassion is born in us...

We humans are made entirely of non-human elements, such as plants, minerals, earth, clouds, and sunshine. For our practice to be deep and true, we must include the ecosystem. If the environment is destroyed, humans will be destroyed. Protecting human life is not possible without protecting the lives of animals, plants, and minerals. The 'Diamond Sutra' teaches us that it is impossible to distinguish between sentient and non-sentient beings. This is one of many ancient Buddhist texts that teach deep ecology...When we appreciate and honor the beauty of life, we will do everything in our power to protect all of life."[32] (Thich Nhat Hanh)

But are we protecting life? Are we the good "stewards" as we are charged to be by the Old Testament of the Bible? The statistics, which reflect our greed, concerning the condition of Mother Earth and her creatures certainly do not reflect good

31 Thich Nhat Hanh, For A Future To Be Possible, Parallax Press. Berkeley. CA. 1993, p.13
32. Ibid. p. 13-19

stewardship:

> "Less that 400 Siberian Tigers are yet surviving in the wild. There are 104 species extinctions per day. It is estimated that by the year 2005, 250 species per day will become extinct. In nine years one third of all species will be lost to our world." (From the Millennium Institute, January 1997

If you have seen the movie, "Seven Years in Tibet," based on the life of Heinrich Harrier, you are acquainted with the scene where the Buddhist Monks move the earthworms from a site where they may be harmed during construction to a place of safety. The explanation for the concern for their safety was that: "They may have been our mother in a previous lifetime." That perspective echoes the Native American philosophy that we are all related. It is also interesting to note that when the Tibetan Monks would walk from place to place, they would strike a walking staff with a circle of bells on the top upon the earth to warn any creatures to move from their path so they should not be harmed. We have seen statues of Buddha, where he holds such a staff.

While we may feel that we are compassionate, caring individuals, are we contributing directly or indirectly to the suffering of our precious animals? In Reiki class, one student said that she had given up eating pork after watching the movie, "Babe". She could not deal with the thought of animals raised to suffer in such tight confined pins, never to see the light of day until they are shoved into trucks for the slaughter. Do we label pigs "pork" and cows "beef" in order to rob them of their soul? Perhaps. Sulak Sivaraksa explains the following:

> "Killing animals and eating meat may be appropriate for a simple agrarian society or village life, but in industrial societies, meat is treated as just another product, and the mass production of meat is not at all respectful of the lives of animals. If people in meat-eating countries could discourage the breeding of animals for consumption, it would not only be compassionate towards the animals, but also towards those human beings in poverty who need grain to survive. There is enough

food in the world to feed us all. Hunger is caused by unequal allocation, and often those who are in need are the food producers."[33]

We must eventually decide that animals are not a "what," but a "who." There was a case in a town in Iowa where two boys murdered several cats with baseball bats. The local press interviewed many people in their community, and one individual declared that this childish prank was not really a crime, since animals do not possess souls. I had to think that maybe this is the same energy, thought, or argument that allowed our young nation to condone slavery and the abuse and genocide of the original Americans. Anyone who is blessed with a loving pet, or a love of animals in general, would certainly argue that animals do indeed possess a soul. It is spiritual blindness or manipulation that would allow us to judge another creature with such harsh discrimination. The mother of the child who was saved from falling into a cage by a gorilla could argue for the soul of gorillas. The household saved by their dog who perished in the home fire could testify that their dog had a soul, a soul that cared enough to give its life to save them. Animals gift us with diversity, joy, love, and a loyalty that surpasses human understanding. I have always maintained that we humans with our intentions and egos have the perspective in reverse. We are not the epitome of evolution, they are. They, who are being evicted by humanity or are electing to leave the planet 100-200 species per day. May the consciousness of humanity be raised before they all leave us alone with our concrete and technology.

I ask that you send Reiki to Mother Earth, Her plants, animals, and minerals, and to the situation of raising the consciousness of humanity on every full moon or more often. We loose approximately 150 acres of farm land each hour 24 hours a day in the United States to development. This does not even include the development of non-agricultural land. Let's put Reiki into raising the consciousness of humanity in designing our

33. Sulak Sivaraksa, "How Societies Can Practice The Precepts", For A Future To Be Possible. by Thich Nhat Hanh, Parallax Press, 1993, p.110

future relationship with Mother Earth. I actually had a dream once where I was on a tour shuttle, and we were moving through a small strip of grass and trees, and a small child asked, "Mommy, what's that stuff?" I knew that the dream was perhaps a reflection of the future where we have grass and trees in limited areas where we can look but not touch, just as we have endangered species now in zoos. I feel that we are indeed living at a critical time to make a difference, and the love, the power, and the Divine Consciousness of Reiki can perhaps assist us to walk and live more lightly on Mother Earth. I will share with you the ancient Cree prophesy:

"Only after the last tree has been cut down. Only after the last river has been poisoned. Only after the last fish has been caught. Only then will you find that money cannot be eaten."

Arthur Waskow wrote a provoking commentary entitled, "What is Eco-Kosher?":

"'Eco-kosher' might as an approach speak to two kinds of Jews--both those who now live by the traditional code of kosher food and those who have decided the traditional code is no longer important to them. It might speak to other communities as well.

"Why does 'eco-kosher' transcend these differences? Because the Earth and the human race are in serious danger. Not economic progress but the way we have pursued economic progress has brought about this danger. For the sake of our children and our children's children, it is crucial to address the issues...

"Torah teaches that if we deny the Earth its Shabbats, (the right to rest) the Earth will make Shabbat anyway--through desolation. The Earth does get to rest. Our only choice is whether the rest occurs with joy or disaster...

"Just as every unique species of plant and animal brings a sacred strand into the sacred web of life, so does the unique wisdom of each human culture. Just as modernity threatens to narrow and crush the diversity of cultures. Both Jews and others are helping to heal that web of life if they give new heart and new life to endangered cultures as well as endangered species."[34]

---

34. Arthur Waskow, "What is Eco-Kosher?" For A Future to Be Possible, Thich Nhat,Hanh, Parallax Press, 1993, p. 116-120

The "Rig Veda" 10.97 states: "The tawny plants were born in the ancient times, three ages before the gods, now I will meditate upon their hundred and seven forms." The "Rig Veda" also defines who a "healer" is in terms of plants: "He in whom the plants gather like kings in an assembly; that priest is called a healer, a slayer of demons, an expeller of disease...The plants have driven out whatever wound was in the body."

There is a Thai Monk named Prajak Kuttajara who was so distressed by the cutting of the ancient trees in northeast Thailand that he decided to ordain the trees as monks in an attempt to save them. After ordination, he would "sash" them by wrapping a yellow cloth, the same color as a monk's robe, around the trunk of the trees. Most loggers, in respect for the Buddhist monks, would not touch the "ordained" trees. The outraged government labeled him as a spiritual outlaw. He replied, "the forest is the source of everything in the world, the dharma, the natural law. It is the university of our life and understanding, the place where we are in relation to nature, but if we practice meditation we will understand ourselves and the relationship between forests and our body." (From The Lost Gospel of the Earth, by Tom Hayden) A similar story comes from the foothills of the Himalayas in India. In 1973, a lumber company was about to cut down trees to make cricket bats. The villagers saved the trees by wrapping their arms around the trees. This event has been labeled the "Chipko (which means embrace) Movement." Master Thich Nhat Hanh says that we can learn from the oak tree:

"In our former lives, we were rocks, clouds, and trees. We may have been an oak tree ourselves. This is not just Buddhist: it is scientific. We humans are a very young species. We appeared on the earth only recently. We were plants, we were trees, and now we have become humans. We have to remember our past existences and be humble. We can learn the Dharma from an oak tree." (From Love In Action by Thich Nhat Hanh)

In Buddhism, there are stories of animals becoming human

and vice versa. In one story, a starving tiger and her cubs spared death by the compassionate sacrifice of a young prince, became disciples of Buddha in their next lifetime. There is a story concerning the lifetimes of Buddha as not always as human. Some stories deal with the transformation of karma and karmic activities according to the various bodies that we have assumed to learn what we need to know to grow spiritually. This particular story of the compassionate gift of the rabbit was translated into a poem called "The Rabbit and the Moon" by the Zen Master Ryokan who lived from 1758-1813. The story goes like this: The God Indra, sovereign of the skies, disguised himself as an old man in need of help. He implored a monkey, a rabbit, and a fox to save his life from starvation. The monkey gathered him nuts to eat, the fox a fish. But the poor desperate rabbit, though he hopped and hopped could find nothing. The others cursed him. The desperate rabbit then had an idea. He told the monkey to gather firewood and the fox to make a fire. He then threw himself into the flames as an offering to the old man. Indra made the rabbit whole again and laid it to rest in the moon in honor of its self-less act.

A story from Hinduism tells of an enlightened old man (an adept) who had the ability to leave his body prior to physical death. The adept, in fact, had to do this in order to remain in an advanced spiritual state of non-attachment to life or death. An adept is a person who "totally understands the Path and has awakened from the dream of 'just eating, working, reproducing, and sleeping.'" [35] He had achieved this ability through the practice of detachment from the physical and therefore relinquishing all karmic ties. One day the adept discovers a helpless fawn in the forest whose mother had been killed by hunters. Rather than allow the fawn to die, he took it home and nurtured it. However, it was nearly beyond appropriate time for the adept to evacuate this physical body, as death was near. Understanding the fate of his actions, the adept chose to re-

---

35. Goswani Kriyananda, A Yoga Dictionary of Basic Sanskrit Terms, The Temple of Krya yoga, Chicago, IL 1966, p. 90

main in the body to care for the fawn. He knowingly gave up his non-attachment in his concern for the welfare of the fawn and died an old man who was trapped by his compassion in an aging body. In his next life, the adept was born a fawn. He assisted other deer in that life, and when he died, he was elevated to a higher spiritual level than he had ever achieved because of his sacrifice and his compassion. That is a contrast or perhaps just another perspective related to the journey in reincarnation of the soul of animals by C. W. Leadbetter:

"When an animal has developed far enough to become human, that means that at the end of his life his soul is not poured back again into the group soul, but remains as a separate entity. And now a very curious but very beautiful fate befalls him. The soul-matter, the water in the vessel becomes itself a vehicle for something much higher, and instead of acting as a soul, it is itself ensouled. We have no exact analogy on the physical plane...The soul of man (woman) is but a partial manifestation of the Divine Spirit. This descent of the ego is symbolized in ancient mythology by the Greek idea of the 'krater' or Cup, and by the mediaeval story of the Holy Grail; for the Grail or the Cup is the perfected result of all that lower evolution , into which is poured the Wine of the Divine Life, so that the soul of man (woman) may be born...The evolution of this soul consists in its gradual return to the higher level on the plane next below the Monadic, carrying with it the result of its descent in the shape of experiences gained and qualities acquired. The physical body should be fully under the control of the soul." (The Masters and the Path, C.W. Leadbeater, p. 18 Theosophical Publishing House, Adyar, India, 1927)

In Siberian Shamanism, animals act as guides to assist with life in the lower, middle, and sometimes (but not often) upper worlds. Some "power animals" can communicate through telepathy, others through speaking, or by signs or signals that such an animal might use to communicate with others. Power animals (and other beings or people) may have the ability to "shape shift"...that is to assume an useful form to accomplish a particular task. In Tibet, such an animal or person might be called a "tulpa":

> "What is a tulpa? A tulpa is a magical creature. The eminent adept of the occult sciences is believed capable, through the strength of his (her) mental concentration, of projecting tulpas in the forms of humans or animals that he utilizes according to his needs, often to execute acts that he himself can only wish for or imagine." (Immortality and Reincarnation, Alexandra David-Neel, p. 87)

According to Hindu philosophy, it is the animals who are great teachers:

> "The lesson of the animals is to understand that we should not be caught in a 'net' by the five senses. These five senses are symbolized by the deer, the elephant, the fish, the moth, and the bee. The deer is lured to his death by soft music made by the hunter. The elephant is caught while rubbing itself against a tree. The moth is brought to its death by its sight, the fish by its taste, and the bee by its sense of smell."[36]

We must remember that the final Precept in Reiki is "Show gratitude to every living thing." We must consider our active role to protect every living thing. Who knows, perhaps in another life, that earthworm was our mother, or we were the oak. We would not ignore someone who was cutting trees in our own back yard, or ruthlessly hunting down our dogs and cats. We would be outraged if someone poured pesticides, sewage, or toxic chemicals into our personal glass of drinking water, or pumping carbon dioxide or other chemicals into the air of your home. I believe that you would immediately do something to stop and/or prevent these activities. Just like a self-treatment in Reiki, a little bit of energy is better than none. That is not to say that you must wrap your arms around trees doomed by the latest strip center. You might consider donating energy in any form to assist.

If you wish to become involved in the preservation of our

sacred land, there is an organization you might contact called the "Boulder Institute for Nature and Human Spirit": 1314 8th St, Boulder, CO 80302, or phone 303-939-8398. You might check the internet for other organizations committed to pre-serving life. I also suggest the following books: <u>Spiritual Ecol-ogy</u>, by Jim Nollman; <u>The Lost Gospel of the Earth</u>; <u>Reclaim-ing the Ecological Wisdom of the Great Traditions</u>, by Tom Hayden; <u>Restoring the Earth, Visionary Solutions from the Bioneers,</u> by Kenny Ausebel, <u>The Soul Unearthed</u>: <u>Celebrat-ing Wilderness and Personal Renewal Through Nature</u>, by Cass Adamas, and <u>Dharma Gaia: Essays in Buddhism and Ecol-ogy</u>, by Allan Badiner.

"Become intimate with your own backyard, with a bit of riverbank, with a pond or hill. The rest of the watershed, the meta-landscape, the conti-nent, planet, and universe will be naturally drawn into this intimacy." John McClellan: <u>The Many Voices of the Boulder Creek Watershed</u>

摩訶般若波羅蜜多心経
觀自在菩薩行深般若波羅蜜多時照見五
蘊皆空度一切苦厄舍利子色不異空空不
異色色即是空空即是色受想行識亦復如
是舍利子是諸法空相不生不滅不垢不淨
不增不減是故空中無色無受想行識無眼
耳鼻舌身意無色声香味觸法無眼界乃至
無意識界無無明亦無無明盡乃至無老死
亦無老死盡無苦集滅道無智亦無得以無
所得故菩提薩埵依般若波羅蜜多故心無
罣礙無罣礙故無有恐怖遠離一切顛倒夢
想究竟涅槃三世諸佛依般若波羅蜜多故
得阿耨多羅三藐三菩提故知般若波羅蜜
多是大神咒是大明咒是無上咒是無等等
咒能除一切苦真実不虛故説般若波羅蜜
多咒即説咒曰
羯諦羯諦 波羅羯諦 波羅僧羯諦 菩提薩婆呵
般若心経

THE HEART SUTRA

MEDITATION ON EMBRACING THE SHADOW

Erich Fromm once said, "Man's main task in life is to give birth to himself." It is so important at this particular time in our Earth history that we learn to love and honor our journey, our desire for spiritual growth and awareness, and respect ourselves for our progression toward greater Light. Once we learn to accept our true worth and value, we can begin to actualize our power and potential in achieving our Soul's Purpose.

It is one of our greatest desires in teaching the Healing Art of Reiki that each person realize the Unconditional Love that they deserve from others as well as from themselves. The EGO may attempt to block such Unconditional Love that flows from the Higher Self. I suggest that if you have difficulty accepting Love from yourself or others, that you consider the following meditation:

EMBRACING THE SHADOW

Close your eyes and relax your body. Breathe in Peace, and Breathe out Light...until you are filled with Peace, and surrounded and protected by the Light. We leave all in Divine Order for the Highest Good.

It is a beautiful day in your thoughts, and you feel the grace and beauty of the world around you. You are walking along a path toward a meadow. This meadow is filled with flowers, and in the distance, you see a tall Oak Tree. As you draw nearer and nearer to this large tree, you realize that it holds the potential for great healing. As you stand facing the tree, call forth the part of you that you find most difficult to accept or embrace. As this aspect of your Rejected or Wounded Self emerges from behind the tree, study it and discern what it is that you find so difficult to accept. What does it look like to you? What is its shape and size? What is its age? Then ask this part of you three questions:
1.) "Where did you come from?"
2.) "Why are you here?" (Or: "What are you teaching me?"
3.) "How can I help you to heal?" (Or: "What do you need to heal?")

Then give this Wounded or Rejected Self a Reiki Treatment, right there under that Oak Tree. Fill that Self with Unconditional Love. Share an affirmation with this Self, such as, "I Love and Accept you no matter what has happened, past, present, or future..." Then draw your awareness back to the present moment, to your breath, and as you breathe in, awaken your senses to the healing power of your own Love.

You may continue this process as many times as you need to for complete healing. It is surprising how many aspects of our Self cry out for Healing Love and attention. This demonstrates basic Karma. We are our own judge and jury, creating parts of ourselves that we can alienate, punish, reject, and condemn into eternity. Better yet, we can choose to embrace, love, and Heal that part of us that keeps us from accepting our own LIGHT. Manifest Light, and know that we who are Reiki love you unconditionally.

"The light that shines beyond the heavens and upon the backs of all, is the same light that is within each person." From The Upanishads

THE FINAL JOURNEY
A Meditation Through the Interdimensional Gate

It is sunset. As you step into the quickening power of the gap between light and dark, yin and yang, you are inspired by the radiant colors of daylight's end. You notice the terra cotta, and the turquoise that surrounds the deep yellow-orange of the setting sun. A hush descends around you as the birds and the wind grow silent and settled for the night. You become aware of the growing stillness and peace within you as well. As the twilight sky begins to darken, you gaze upward at the first evening star's light in the ancient heavens. It is here that our journey begins; our journey from your birth into individuality through the essence of the dimension of time and space.

Your spirit is drawn to your own first star. When you separated from the One Great Golden Light, you migrated as an independent soul to the vibration of your new home. Move now to that place, your original home. Go there now, return to your home as it was and when it was that you were there. Go to the birthing chamber, the Chamber of Light. This is the place where your vibration is calibrated to accept the form that you will need here. The lights are glowing brighter now and you feel the confines of this chamber opening now to the light outside of it. Sense and feel those around you waiting outside this sacred chamber. These are beings of Light and Love who have come to assist you in your journey into first being. As you emerge from the Chamber of Light, you are in First Life. The beings of Light assist you in learning all that you need to know about adjusting pure spirit to a physical being-ness. They show you a still, blue pond that reflects your Divine Image back to you. See, sense, and feel how you look. Gaze at the sky above you. How does it look to you from your new perspective? Is there Light or darkness in that sky? Look at your new home. Experience all that you need to know of this First Mystery. Bring forward the memories of the ancient secrets and revelations of First Life. The First Mystery represents the Root Chakra; the initiation into materiality.

The Second Mystery leads you through time, space, and interdimensional reality to the Crystal Healing Chamber of Atlantis. To enter into the Earth's vibratory frequency, you must make a choice: male or female. The left gate opens to the mysteries of the feminine, the right to the masculine. Sense the initial gate that you are choosing for your soul in that incarnation. The Keeper of the Mysteries appears before you at the moment that you choose. Open your heart to the power of this mystery. Why have you chosen your gender to enhance your soul's purpose in Atlantis? The Second Mystery represents the Sacral Center. Experience your life in Atlantis; visit the site of the blue crystal, the twelve crystal skulls, the hall of records. Where are these mysteries now? Remember other mysteries. Is there anything that needs healed from that lifetime? If so, heal it now if it is in Divine Order.

Feel yourself traveling forth now to the Ancient Valley of the Kings in Egypt. You must now experience death of the ego-self to learn of your limitless power. This Third Mystery is represented by the energy of the Solar Plexus Center. Enter the pyramid through the sacred gate of initiation. First you descend as the blackness consumes you. Your heart is free of fear as you emerge into the chamber of the sarcophagus. The priest is waiting there for you. You are attuned to the ancient mysteries that preclude the death of the ego. You lie down in the deep stone bed and are covered by the priest. For three days you are left alone with your breath in the darkness. Reflect upon all that you learned there about shedding the ego like the skin of the powerful serpent. You are born anew, healed and whole, as the priest of Luxor removes the covering of the sarcophagus. Your power that the ego once hid from you has now been restored and illuminated. See, sense, and feel the symbol of that power in the gift that the priest now presents to you. You are wrapped in a white robe and introduced to Ra, the god of the Egyptian sun, the insurer of life. Feel this illumination throughout your being. As male or female, you insure life as well. It serves your soul's purpose to endure as human and to share that Light of life with prodigy. We rest and reflect now upon that ultimate mystery of the creation of new life.

JOURNEY, PART TWO

It is time to communicate the mystery of the Grail. For it is said that the cup which captured the draining blood of Christ rests deep within a well in Glastonbury, England. Is this not fitting that Galstonbury has been called by some the physical location of the Heart Center of the Earth? That vibration leads us to the awareness of the Grail hidden deep within our own heart; the sacred place where the blood of Christ and other great Masters flow. I believe the color of the Grail Cup itself is green, representing the emerald green magnified in the Heart Center. Journey in you heart now to Glastonbury, and gaze deep into that sacred well that shelters the Grail. The Grail initiates within the wellspring of our own heart the energy of ultimate compassion.

We move back in time to the ancient Healing Center of

Asclepius, the Greek god of healing. There we also find Chiron, his teacher, the ancient Centaur. Asclepius approaches you with his long cloak and staff with coiled serpent. It is time to awaken within you the heart's secret hidden in the Throat Center, for spoken words have great power. There are vibrations within the Throat Center that can manifest the Highest Good, or cast the longest shadow of darkness. If you are ready to reawaken this slumbering power to manifest goodness and Light, you may choose to drink the blue vial that he now presents to you. It contains liquid Light. As you drink of it, feel and sense the swirling warmth in your throat as that compassionate, Kotama energy is released in your throat. Asclepius teaches us that we now hold a great healing potential in the vibratory frequency within our own voice, the healing power of the spoken word.

In our dreams we visit the Himalayan Mountains of Tibet. It is the early days of high vibration just after the rising out of the water. From the influence of the minerals of water, high vibrational caves were formed. There exists in Tibet a most sacred cave. As you enter, you smell the sandalwood and glimpse the Thangkas and the golden bowls used in secret ceremony. The secrets and mysteries have been hidden deep in this sacred cave, protected from the darkness that might attempt to pervert its use for lesser light purposes. We have also hidden our secrets in the dark cave of our Third Eye to protect them from the rest of the world in fear of judgment. We have also hidden our Thangkas and our golden bowl which contains the mystical energy of the Mastership. An ancient Tibetan lama is there to assist you in learning to trust enough to reveal these secrets to you. You must ask this ancient one to initiate and open your Third Eye. He leads you deeper within the sacred cave of Insight and Intuition for this sacred rite. You are seated in a circle of white candles. Sandalwood fills your senses. You are invited into a deep meditation with this lama. You become aware of the energy of his aura intensifying, radiating, filling you with Divine Light. There is an explosion of Light in your Third Eye. You see, sense, and feel a crystal pyramid illuminating and casting prisms of light through all chakras and bodies of your being. Your gift of mystical intuition is restored to you. You bow to the lama as you leave this high place of ancient secrets and spiritual revelations.

The River Ganges flows through the soul of India. It is here that we enter into the stream of our own Divine Consciousness at the Crown Center. This sacred water represents the Wisdom of the Spirit to us in our journey. As you step into this holy water, we are reminded that the Earth Herself is a spiritual being living a physical life. Our spirit flows into the physical to enhance our compassion and realize our soul's purpose, just as Hers does. We join with Her here and our two journeys become one. The water of the sacred River Ganges teaches us that we are one with the Earth and all that exists or ever existed here. Rest now in the shallow, gentle warmth of the flowing water of the River Ganges. Become the water of the spirit.

JOURNEY THREE

The Soul Star Chakra moves us beyond the Earth Plane. Just as the Soul Star exists beyond the body, our journey leads us beyond the Earth to the Seven Sisters, the Pleiades. Each of the axis chakras is represented by one of the Seven Sisters. The Soul Star represents a bridge to our life prior to this one and all others on Earth. Visit the Ray of the Seventh Sister of the Pleiades, who initiates you into the awareness of Interdimensional Planes of existence. She holds up a shimmering holographic mirror so you may see all aspects, all sides of your Intedimensional Self, past, present, and future, for all are one. The Ray of the Seventh Sister teaches you that you may view others in your Transformational healing work with these same holographic eyes, seeing the source of dis-ease in order to accelerate the healing process within each individual.

We now move back in time to the Founding Energies of our solar system: Lyra. The Founders have been waiting for you to illustrate the mysteries of the origins of Tao, of all energy that cannot be labeled or named. For that which can be labeled or named is not the Tao. Golden Light surrounds you and influences your aura to a higher vibration. Sense, feel, and know that you are melting into the finer frequency of the Tao. All is Tao, and Tao is all. And like a Great Circle coming back unto itself, you are returned to a pinpoint of Light at the center of that Circle. This is the **bindu**, the invisible point of the end and yet the point from which everythng originates.

The pinpoint of Light grows as you are drawn into its vortex. The Golden Circle, you suddenly realize, is a sphere, rather than a circle, of infinite energy that surrounds you. At the center of that sphere, at that pinpoint of White Light, lies the Interdimensional Center. It is Shambala. The Great Masters of Shambala open the etheric gates and you enter in. Everything is white, as it contains all colors, all 144,000 infinite frequencies of Infinite Light. In Shambala, you are taught that life has no beginning and no end. Matter can neither be created nor destroyed. This is the mystery of all mysteries. This is the Master Mystery, for inside of you is the key to All. For those who have ears to hear, let them hear and understand All now.

Om Shambala, Om Shambala, Om Shambala
Gate, Gate, Paragate, Parasamgate, Bodi Svaha.

Note: The "Gate" is from the Heart Sutra and means: "Gone, gone, gone beyond, gone wholly beyond--Enlightenment!"

Make room for yourself inside yourself. Rumi

THE FIVE ANCIENT TIBETAN RITES
OF REJUVENATION

The following information is paraphrased from the pamphlet, "The Eye of Revelation" by Peter Kelder:

"There are Seven Psychic Vortexes in the body. Vortex A is located in the forehead, B is in the posterior part of the brain, C is in the region of the throat at the base of the neck, Vortex E is located in the reproductive anatomy and is directly connected with C. Vortexes F and G are located in each knee. These Psychic Vortexes revolve at great speed. When they are revolving at high speed and at the same rate of speed the body is in perfect health. When one or more of them slow down, old age, loss of power, and senility set in."

These excercises are designed to start and accelerate the vortex spinning.

The First Rite involves spinning clockwise. Stand erect and simply raise your arms to a horizontal position, level with your shoulders, keeping your finger tips as close together as possible. Then spin your body clockwise until you are slightly dizzy. (Visualize a clock on the floor at your feet and spin in the direction that the hands would move.) This stimulates Vortexes A, B, and E.

For Rite Number Two, lie down on your back with your hands next to your hips, finger tips close together and pointed slightly toward each other. On the inhale of the breath, raise your legs until they are vertical or slightly over center and your head chin to the chest. On the exhale, lower legs and head slowly to the floor. If you can't raise your legs, raise the knees to vertical letting the feet hang down. Repeat with the breath.

Rite Three: Kneel with your knees a little less than shoulder width apart and your toes curled forward. Place your hands with finger tips together, on the back of the thighs, put your chin on your chest. On the inhale lean back as far as possible, lifting and stretch your head back as far as you can. Now exhale as you bring your head back to chin on your chest and straighten your body to vertical. Repeat with the breath. Accelerates Votexes E, and C.

Rite Number Four: This is sometimes called the "Table Top". Sit with your legs extended in front of you, toes pointed upward. Place your hands on the floor at your hips, fingertips together, and pointed toward your feet, chin on your chest. On the inhale raise the body so that the legs, from the knees down are vertical and the body is horizontal, extend the head as far back as you can. As you exhale, lower the body to the original sitting position, with your chin on your chest. Repeat with the breath. Stimulates vortexes F, G, E, and C.

Rite Number Five: In Yoga part of this is the Cobra position and the second part is the Downward Facing Dog. Lie on the floor face down, your hands beside your shoulders, fingertips together, your feet about hip width apart, on your toes. For the starting position, push your shoulders up off the floor and arch your spine, your head should be extended back, gently, as far as you can. (This is the Cobra.) On the inhale push your hips up as far as possible, bring the chin to the chest. (This is Downward Facing Dog.) On the exhale bring your body slowly to the Cobra position. Then again on the inhale back into the Downward Facing Dog. Keep repeating.

There is a sixth Rite, however it is reserved for those who choose to live a celibate lifestyle.

When we were trained in these Rites, we were also given affirmations to use in conjunction with these Rites. The history as we were told was that these Rites were part of the monastic rituals practiced by Tibetan Monks throughout history. They were brought forward to us by a German woman who had visited a monastery in Germany.

TIBETAN RITE AFFIRMATIONS

1. I breathe deep, silent and relaxed. (on the inhale)
   I release lesser light energy. (on the exhale)

2. I breathe deep, silent and relaxed. (on the inhale)
   I'm living from my center. (on the exhale)

3. I breathe deep, silent and relaxed. (on the inhale)
   Endless energy flows through my body. (on the exhale)

4. I breathe deep, silent and relaxed. (on the inhale)
   I am powerful and alive. (on the exhale)

5. I breathe deep, silent and relaxed. (on the inhale)
   I am young, I stay young and dynamic. (on the exhale)

Rite #1

Rite #2

Rite #3

Rite #4

Rite #5

CREATING SACRED SPACE INSIDE AND OUT

We create sacred space with our intention to do so. After smudging, or clearing of energies (with Reiki Symbols) in a given area, we can then allow our physical Self the task of setting appropriate boundaries for our sacred space. One way to do this is to gather stones (with their permission to serve) into a sacred circle. A circle has no beginning and no end. You may choose to create a circle of stones that are significant to you, such as crystals, chakra stones, or amethyst, or you may choose to create a sacred circle based upon the ancient wisdom of the Medicine Wheel.

With the Medicine Wheel, we will begin by placing our sacred stones clockwise from a position at the North (the mental), to the East (the spiritual), to the South (the emotional), to the west (the physical). Traditionally, the stone to the North is white, as north is the place of contemplation, stillness, winter, and snow.

Always ask permission of the stone before moving or touching it. If it chooses to serve you in creating sacred space, then speak sacred words as you place the white stone in the position of the North. This will awaken the sacred spirit of the stone to collect and anchor sacred space. You may also feel compelled to utilize a symbol as you place the stone where it needs to be. The second stone is yellow, and it is placed in the East. The East is the place of the rising sun, of renewal, and we honor the sun's presence in our lives with this yellow stone. Once again, and with all, speak sacred words and/or use symbols as you position the stone. The stone to the South is red, the place of fire, of transformation. To the West we place a black stone, the place of the setting sun, of darkness and rest. After you have invoked and anchored the sacred stones, you may then set about whatever purpose you may have: Absentia Healing, meditation, self healing, or sacred ceremony. I always invite my guides from the highest light to be with me on any such occasion.

If you are in a situation where stones are not available, you may choose to create or anchor sacred space with whatever is available to you: drops of water or Reiki Symbols placed in a circle, pillows, a blanket, chairs, or whatever you may desire that sets you and this space apart from the rest of the world.

I also suggest that you create a sacred table, place, or shelf at home (or at work) that is for the purpose of holding objects that are sacred to you. One enterprising young mother said that she bought a glass cheese dome to place over her sacred objects, and explained to her young children that this space was hers alone. (Later she bought each of her children one as well.) Sacred space is a haven for our spiritual practices and sacred objects. We can be at peace there, building on the exterior what we eventually manifest inside of us.

White Light Symbol

SIDDHI

There are beneficial side effects that come from walking a spiritual path, regardless of which one you are on. These have been considered "occult powers," and are not to be pursued as a means to an end, however they may appear in this life as a result of past-life karma. No spiritual practice or aspiration is ever a wasted effort. Remember that life is continuous.

There are said to exist eight "siddhis" which may manifest as a result of devoted spiritual practice:

1.) To become very large at will.
2.) To become very small at will.
3.) To become very heavy at will.
4.) To become very light at will.
5.) To manifest desire.
6.) To obtain anything.
7.) To control anything.
8.) Mastery to direct affairs by using the elements.

It is understood that a certain level of consciousness must be achieved in the Universal consideration of these powers, as they can only be used by those who would not abuse them.

There are also a list of powers and wisdom, according to Sri Patanjali, which come as a result of advanced meditation practices:

1.) Knowledge of the past events and future happenings
2.) Understanding creature sounds
3.) Power of mind over matter
4.) Knowledge of one's past lives
5.) Knowing the moment of death
6.) Understanding the meaning of all symbols
7.) Clairaudience
8.) Clairsentience
9.) Clairvoyance
10.)Astral projection
11.)Projection of action of the mind (Kriya)

Through the process of your Transformation, you may be presented with many gifts and opportunities. They come as a result of dissolving potential or dormant karma, and the forwarding of good karmic effects from past life experiences. Gifts inherent in further healing empowerment through the process of Transformational Reiki are the gifts of good health, peace, contentment, and detachment from the drama of life around you. You have the ability to become the Buddha who meditates in the mouth of the serpent. You have the ability to transcend and transform suffering into positive healing potential, for yourself and then others.

Blessings to you on your Divine Path to Kokora, your Heart Mind which opens the doors of Universal Compassion!

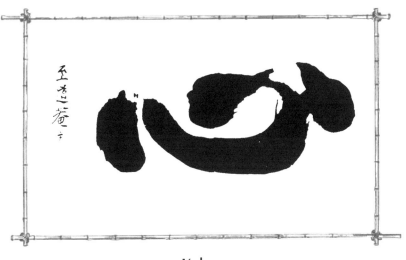

KOKORA

In Gratitude

It is with deepest gratitude that I express my appreciation for all Beings who assisted with bringing forth the sacred teachings and mysteries herein contained. I ask for continued Blessings for all involved, including Steven Mitchell, Robert Tentinger, Master Thich Nhat Hanh, Choa Kok Sui, Sogyal Rinpoche, Pema Chodron, Pandit Rajmani Tigunait, and His Holiness the Fourteenth Dalai Lama, a "simple monk".

From the book <u>Kundun</u>, by Mary Craig:

"IN my lifetime conditions will be as they are now, peaceful and quiet. But the future holds darkness and misery. I have warned you of these things." The last political Testament of the Thirteenth Dalai Lama

"A small child running out of a burning building is powerless to put the fire out by himself. All he can do is yell, 'Fire', in the hope that some bigger, stronger people will listen and take action. That's exactly what we Tibetans are doing. Our home is disintegrating and our relatives are in there." Tendzin Choegyal, younger brother of the Dalai Lama

"All is not lost. We Tibetans are resilient, patient, and resourceful. Ours is a just cause. We continue to be confident that truth will ultimately triumph and our land and people will once more be free. Would the Chinese consider the Tibetan question so sensitive if our cause was dead? Under difficult circumstances we have kept the Tibetan spirit and sense of hope alive. However, it is clear that these efforts alone will not be sufficient to bring about a final positive solution. Therefore, I appeal to readers of this book to support the Tibetan people, so that ultimately they may again live in peace and dignity." His Holiness the Dalai Lama

Reiki Mystery School™ Class offerings: The mystery teachings that transcend this book; the mysteries that we share in a class that are too sacred for any book.

<u>CLASS DAY ONE: TRANSFORMATIONAL REIKI ™</u>

This class is for the serious aspirant of the Reiki Path, and the prerequisite is Reiki Level II. We share the secrets of Reiki as a healing art. The ancient roots of Reiki are revealed to assist in the dynamic process of healing and spiritual growth. Rites related to enlightenment, immortality, and rejuvenation are offered. We study the Tibetan perspective of disease as related to karmic actions. The Ancient Tibetan Fire Attunement that links the Soul to Interdimensional Reality and Soul's Purpose is offered. This increases the vibrational rate and healing empowerment within the individual. In this class, you are introduced to color healing and the Interdimensional Chakra System and Interdimensional Bodies that activate deeper healing in the physical body. You learn of a healing field called the Unisonium, where practitioner and healee meet to create a more intense energy potential for healing. Meditations in class include: Meeting your Interdimensional Guide; Interdimensional Chakras; Planes of Existence; Soul's Purpose; and melting into the Unisonium. This day focuses upon increasing student empowerment.

<u>CLASS DAY TWO: KOTAMA: THE WORD ™</u>

Kotama is the application of Sacred Sound. We use sacred Mantras and seven powerful scripts to assist in healing each of the seven Bodies: Physical, Mental, Emotional, Spiritual, Light, Cosmic, and Interdimensional.

Advanced Healing Techniques for self and others will be an integral part of the Kotama Teachings. Such techniques include specific hand placements to activate a pulse in the Meridian System that opens a gateway to each of the seven Bodies. This pathway encourages deeper healing and release of old patterns that exist from this and other lifetimes as related to karma and disease. Four ancient symbols are shared including the symbols for manifesting, increasing energy, compassion, and a symbol to disperse negative energies in yourself and others. You receive the Tibetan Mandala of Protection. This day focuses upon utilizing your increased power to help others heal more effectively.

Guided Meditation Tapes

© Karyn Mitchell, Ph.D, N.D.

Most tapes approximately 50 minutes in length, $10.00 Each

REIKI TAPES AVAILABLE:

What Is Reiki?/ Reiki Meditation:
> What Reiki is and does, Precepts and Principles of Reiki. Side two is a meditation.

Experience Reiki.
> How a Reiki Treatment might feel as each chakra is brought into harmony. Experiential.

Absentee Healing/Self Healing:
> Level II practitioners & up. Techniques for self & Absentia Healing.

Vertical Reiki.
> (Two Volume Set $20.) Meditations & Healing with Client Standing. Master Usui's Method Without a Table.

Meeting the Grand Masters:
> Advanced Spiritual Journey to meet Usui, Hayashi, & Takata.

SPIRITUAL ADVANCEMENT TAPES:

Meditation for Spiritual Advancement:
> The next step. A quantum leap in spiritual growth.

Soul Star Meditation/Soul Beyond the River:
> Anchoring energies in the chakra beyond the crown center; Finding the first you to incarnate upon planet Earth..

Journey to the Tao Chakra/Moving Into Light:
> From the Crown to the Soul Star to the "Tao" Chakra, the golden center. Ever dreamed of being pure Light?

Finding Your Soul's Purpose:
> Why have you chosen to be born at this time? Meet special guides.

Depossession as Therapy:
> Based on the Unquiet Dead by Edythe Fiore. Recognize symptoms, & release energies.

Gentle Depossession.
> For therapists & Healers. Karyn Mitchell's technique for releasing energies.

The Emerald, The Eagle, The River, & You.
> Advanced mystical meditation with much symbolism.

Find Your Spirit Guides:
> A tape to help you meet those Guides and Masters who help you.

Healing Your Past:
> A life Regression to heal pain & trauma in the present. Inner Child work.

Past Life Regression As Therapy:
> What it is, how it heals. A regression is included.

Advanced Past Life Techniques:
> The Destiny Train & Portrait Gallery, for groups or individuals.

Self Hypnosis/Feng Shui The Spirit

Atlantis, Lemuria & Space:
    Regression to the life before your Earth Journey.
Abductions: How, When, & Why?
     Tape based on a workshop Karyn teaches throughout the U.S. (The Book, ABDUCTIONS, STOP THEM, HEAL THEM, NOW is $9.95)
Past Life Relationships:
    Find a present love in a past life.
White Light Cobalt Tetrahedran/Two Invocations
        White Light-InterdimensionalJourney to gain the Cosmic
        Tetrahedran for protection. Two Invocations for healing dis-ease
        and releasing fear.
Interdimensional Chakra Meditation/ Interdimensional Journey
        Journey through the Interdimensional Chakras.
Healing the Child Within:
    Heal your wounded child, and learn what secrets this child holds for you.
A Bridge of Light and Transition
        The dying Process and beyond.

HEALING TAPES:

Asthma:
    Three emotional reasons for asthma, and how to heal them.
Smoking Cessation:
    Three strong meditations for freedom from smoking.
Weight Reduction:
    How to achieve and maintain your ideal weight by healing the root cause of the situation.
Ayurvedic Weight:
    Based on the book PERFECT WEIGHT by Deepak Chopra. Body types & balance techniques
Soul Retrieval:
    Shamanic & Hypnotherapy techniques for restoring the whole soul.
Cancer & Chemotherapy:
     If this is the course of action chosen, then ease the pain of "conventional treatment".
Healing the Heart
     Meditations for coronary healing & stress release.
Healing the Cells of the Body:
    Using Light, color, and the River of Ki to flow through the body for healing.
Chakra Health:
    Cleansing the Chakras and fill them with energy from the Highest Light. Spin/open chakras. Grounding.
NOTE: ALL TAPES ARE CREATED & COPYRIGHTED BY KARYN MITCHELL. MUST NOT BE DUPLICATED OR COPIED.

Midwest International University
for Holistic & Spiritual Education
Offers Degree Programs in the Following Areas:

- Bachelor of Transpersonal Psychology
- Master of Transpersonal Psychology
- Doctor of Philosophy in Transpersonal Psychology
- Doctor of Theology
- Doctor of Naturopathic Medicine

Call 815-732-9047 for a Catalog

Karyn and Steven Mitchell travel and teach Reiki, TransReiki®, Advanced Reiki Techniques, Melody Crystal Healing, Hynotherapy, and Ministerial Classes throughout the World. For speaking and teaching engagements or to sponser a class, please contact:

Steven Mitchell,
Haven Center for Healing & Education
603 Geneva Rd., St. Charles, IL 60174
815-732-7150

e-mail mitchell@essex1.com

Karyn K. Mitchell, N.D., Ph.D.
Biography

Karyn Mitchell is a Naturopathic Doctor with a Ph.D in Psychology. She has attended The University of Iowa, The University of Nebraska, Loras College, Buena Vista College, Midwest University, and Westbrook. She is an international teacher and speaker in the fields of Reiki, Hypnotherapy, Vegetarian Lifestyle, Meditation, Natural Medicine, and Shamanism. She has been a student of Psychology, Metaphysics, Religion, and Philosophy for over thirty years. She is a member of the American Naturopathic Medical Association. She has taken the Five Mindfulness Trainings with Master Thich Nhat Hanh, a Buddhist Monk ordained in the Zen tradition, and has taken initiations and studied with His Holiness the Dalai Lama. Also, Karyn is a graduate of the Silva Method, and has studied Shamanism with Michael Harner and Sandra Ingerman (The Foundation for Shamanic Studies). She has studied other cultural dimensions of Shamanism in other countries and from other instructors. She is a medical intuitive and mystic dedicated to sharing the spirit of compassion and love for people, animals, plants, and minerals.

She is a Holistic Counselor and a Certified Reiki Master-Teacher of the Usui Shiki Ryoho School of Reiki. She is certified through the American Board of Hypnotherapy as an Instructor of Metaphysical Hypnotherapy, and is an instructor certified by the International Medical Dental Hypnotherapy Association (I.M.D.H.A.), and the American Association of Behavioral Therapists. Karyn holds further certification from the National Association for Transpersonal Psychology in the areas of Clinical Hypnotherapy, Transpersonal Therapy, Analytical Hypnotherapy, and Past Life Regression Therapy. She and her husband, Steven Mitchell have co-founded A.R.T., the Association for Regression Therapists, and "Reiki Path" School of Reiki Instruction. They have both devoted their life's work to assisting others with their spiritual growth. Karyn maintains an office at Haven Holistic Center in St. Charles, Illinois and works as a Holistic Counselor, Naturopath, Reiki Practitioner, Teacher, and Regression Therapist. She has taught at two high schools and three universities in the United States. Her personal spiritual philosophy is to guide students and clients to a place of personal awareness and empowerment.

Her books, <u>REIKI A TORCH IN DAYLIGHT</u>, <u>REIKI BEYOND THE USUI SYSTEM</u>, <u>REIKI MYSTERY SCHOOL</u>, <u>WALK-INS/SOUL EXCHANGE</u>, and <u>SACRED TRUTH/THE BLOODLINE OF SOPHIA</u> published by Mind Rivers, are available at most book stores.

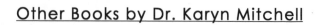

Other Books by Dr. Karyn Mitchell

Reiki: A Torch in Daylight
ISBN# 0-9640822-1-7
Retail $14.95

Reiki Beyond the Usui System
ISBN# 0-9640822-2-5
Retail $19.96

Walk-Ins/Soul Exchange
ISBN# 0-9640822-4-1
Retail $17.95

The Sacred Truth
The Bloodline of Sophia
ISBN# 0-9640822-9-2
Retail $ 18.95

Call 815-732-7150 for Ordering
Information
Retail/Wholesale